The Yellow Wallpaper

The Screenplay

Based on the works of
Charlotte Perkins Gilman

Written by

Aric Cushing and Logan Thomas

DEDICATION

This book is dedicated to every cast and crew member that helped in the making of this film, before and after.

"In homes we were all born. In homes we all die, or hope to die."
Charlotte Perkins Gilman

As written down by Aric Cushing in his journal, in the year of 1989.
17 years before pre-production began.

ACKNOWLEDGEMENT

WITHOUT CHARLOTTE PERKINS GILMAN,
NONE OF THIS WOULD HAVE BEEN POSSIBLE.

i

Logan on set.

THE YELLOW WALLPAPER

CREDITS ROLL OVER:

The blighted, desolate plains of the American
West.

The giant red sun rises over the horizon, filling
the frame with fire.

The year is 1894.

                                        CUT TO:

EXT. MOUNTAIN GROVE. DAY.

People move through the charred remains of
houses. Chimneys still stand, strange pillars of
brick amidst the blackened, scorched wood.

An OLD WOMAN pokes through the remains with a
stick.

A man, JOHN WEILAND, stands and stares at the
smoldering fire. His face hangs from shock, black
smudges spackle his face.

John Weiland is a thirty five year old physician,
of wise features, with small spectacles, brown
receding hair and a medium frame.

Behind him, bodies move like ghosts.

A woman wanders through the evidence of her
destroyed house, weeping.

John surveys the destruction.

                                          CUT TO:

ONE WEEK LATER.

EXT. DIRT ROAD. DAY.

A carriage rumbles over the dirt road.

JENNIE GASKELL, sister to CHARLOTTE WEILAND, sits in the back seat. She holds her sister's face in her chest, as Charlotte weeps uncontrollably. Both women are turned away, their faces hidden.

John sits in the carriage with the women. He stares out the window, disengaged.

                                          CUT TO:

EXT. ROAD. DAY.

Mist crawls low as the trees hang heavily.

A black carriage moves under a canopy of branches.

                                          CUT TO:

EXT. WAKEFIELD HOUSE. DAY.

MR. HENDRICKS, bank solicitor, walks with John around the house.

                    MR. HENDRICKS
          The house is full. You can add
          anything you like, but please do
          not take anything with you.

                    JOHN
          We do not have anything.

Mr. Hendricks laughs, gently. John is nervous and
exhausted.

                    MR. HENDRICKS
          That's fine.

                    JOHN
          Have you worked for the Wakefields
          very long, Mr. Hendricks?

                    MR. HENDRICKS
          Isaac.

                    JOHN
          Isaac.

                    MR. HENDRICKS
          Oh yes. It is always difficult.   .   .
          Finding the right people. But I can
          tell that you are different. Good
          folk.   .   .

                    JOHN
          Thank you.

                    MR. HENDRICKS
          You saw the dry lake bed; we passed it
          On the way here. You can use it, as a
          Short cut, back to town. (beat)   It
          Will be about twenty five minutes.
          Walking, that is.   .   .

                    JOHN
          I can only pay you for two months.   .
          up front.

> MR. HENDRICKS
> No, no. One month is fine. (beat)
> Oh yes. I would not try to grow any-
> thing. This ground is dead.

                                    CUT TO:

Jennie and Charlotte sit in the carriage in the
distance.

SHOT THROUGH THE GLASS OF THE HORSE CARRIAGE:

CHARLOTTE WEILAND sits in the passenger seat. Her
jet black hair is bundled up on her head, as is
the fashion of the time, and her soot covered
dress folds about her. Her face is stark and
angular. She is mid to late thirties

> JENNIE O.C.
> It's larger than I thought.

Charlotte opens the door and steps out of the
carriage.

JENNIE GASKELL follows her sister. Jennie is 44
and extremely thin. She has a tough, angular

features and a wizened face.

Jennie reaches down and sifts her hand through the dirt. She examines it for richness.

                                        CUT TO:

CLOSE UP

of Charlotte as she turns towards the house. She has a strange beauty, with a long thin neck and delicate features.

                                        CUT TO:

EXT. FRONT PORCH OF WAKEFIELD HOUSE. DAY.

John turns the corner with Mr. Hendricks.

                MR. HENDRICKS
        Well.

Mr. Hendricks fishes into his pocket and pulls out a key.

                MR. HENDRICKS (cont'd)
        Here you are.

                JOHN
        Oh. Yes.

Jennie and Charlotte stand back on the porch, the house looming behind them.

                MR. HENDRICKS
            (looking out)
        It's all done then.

                JOHN
        If you want to take the carriage back, it is already paid for—

                    MR. HENDRICKS
                   (tipping his hat)
          No. I always walk. Ladies.

John, Charlotte and Jennie watch as Mr. Hendricks
turns and walks away.

                                        CUT TO:

INT. ENTRYWAY. DAY.

WE MOVE INTO THE house with John, Jennie, and
Charlotte.

Dust sparkles in the rays of sunlight falling
through the tall windows. It is a cavernous
entrance. The foyer is large, with massive wooden
doors that slide shut on all sides. The walls are
covered with paintings and tapestries, all one

upon another.

John, Charlotte, and Jennie stand dwarfed in the expanse.

>   JOHN
>   Well?

>   JENNIE
>   What first?

>   CHARLOTTE
>   I think a bedroom. I need to lie
>   down.

                                        CUT TO:

INT. FIRST HALLWAY. DAY.

John, Charlotte, and Jennie's shoes **clunk** over the wood floor.

John opens the door to a room.

They step inside.

                                        CUT TO:

INT. JENNIE'S ROOM. DAY.

Jennie runs her hand along the blanket of the bed.

The room is simple and conservative. And drab. A chest of drawers against the wall, a single bed, and a standing closet.

John and Charlotte stand in the doorway as Jennie does to the closet.

                    JENNIE
          It looks like the maid's quarters.

Charlotte turns and exits the room.

                    JOHN
          If you don't like it, this is
          perfectly. .   (John watches
          Charlotte exit) fine for us. We
          can take it. . .

                    JENNIE
          No. I didn't mean it.

                                        CUT TO:
INT. LIBRARY. DAY.

The stuck door groans then cracks open.

John and Jennie move inside.

The library is revealed in a shocking display of
brooding shadow and mahogany. The walls are
stacked with dusty books and animal heads.

                                        CUT TO:

INT. JOHN AND CHARLOTTE'S ROOM. DAY.

Charlotte moves into the main bedroom. She
crosses the deep gold carpet and--

Sits on the bed.

WE PULL IN

to her from behind as she reaches for something
in her pocket. She pulls out tiny, crumpled
pieces of paper, covered with writing. She looks
down to the fragile pages.

                                        CUT TO:

INT. LIBRARY. DAY.

Jennie sits on the sofa. A large fireplace looms
behind her.

                    JENNIE
          There may be some flour, but I would
          Be surprised if there is much of any-
          thing else.

                    JOHN
          I'm really not very hungry.

John looks through the books.

                    JOHN (cont'd)
          I don't think Charlotte will want to
          eat.

                    JENNIE
               (hit of exhausted sarcasm)
          Well, if Charlotte's not hungry, and
          you're not hungry, and I'm not hungry.
          I suppose there is no need to make
          dinner then.

                    JOHN
               (looking at her)
          I suppose not.

                    JENNIE
          Tell me, how long did that man say it
          had been since the last people lived
          here?
                    JOHN
          Six months. Why?

11

>   JENNIE
> I find it strange that the house is
> covered in dust, but the plants are
> cell watered.
>
>   JOHN
> I suppose.

John lost in his book—

After a moment, he looks up.

John just catches a glimpse of Jennie's head
moving through the door as the door closes.

John sits down on the sofa and begins to cry.

                              CUT TO:

INT. JOHN AND CHARLOTTE'S ROOM. NIGHT.

John undoes his suspenders and begins to take off
his shirt.

Charlotte is curled in bed, facing the window.
She stares forward.

After a moment, John gets into bed. John lies
next to her. He curls up and watches the back of
Charlotte's head.

He turns away from her, and says nothing.

                              CUT TO:

INT. FIRST HALLWAY. NIGHT.

Jennie emerges from the sewing room and closes
the door. She moves down the hallway. She douses
out the large oil lamps hanging from the ceiling

with a metal extension.

The library door squeaks open.

An amber glow flickers from the room.

Jennie turns—

She goes to the door and slowly pushes it open.

                    JENNIE
          John?

                                        CUT TO:

INT. LIBRARY. NIGHT.

Jennie steps into the room.

HOLD ON the library.

Jennie moves through the room.

Spooked, Jennie goes to the lamp. It illuminates
the centerpiece portrait of the library: a
massive painting of what appears to be a Dutch
merchant.

Jennie leans down and reads the metal tag name on
the painting. It is too dirty to make out. Jennie
rubs her finger over the tag.

It reads—

ECKHART VAN WAKEFIELD.

                                        CUT TO:

INT. WAKEFIELD HOUSE. DINING ROOM. NEXT DAY.

CLOSE UP

Bowl of oats.

> JENNIE
> There were oats left.

John stares down at the oats.

Jennie sits down at the table with her bowl.

Charlotte weakly picks up her spoon.

> JENNIE (cont'd)
> (passionless)
> I'm going to do a thorough cleaning
> today to see what we've gotten
> ourselves into.

> JOHN
> Fine. I'll go into town and see what
> they have for work.

> JENNIE
> Do you mean patients?

> JOHN
> Patients, labor. Whatever I can get.

> JENNIE
> It's only been little more than a
> week.

> JOHN
> How long should I wait?

> CHARLOTTE
> But you. . . are a professional
> John. You shouldn't take just any
> job.

14

                    JOHN
          Well, she shouldn't have kept our
          money in the house. You didn't want
          to put it in a bank so. . . I
          will take whatever I can find now.

Charlotte shrinks in her chair.

                    JOHN (cont'd)
          What little jack loaned us will not
          Get us very far.

Jennie gets up from the table angry.

                    JENNIE
          As long as you're going into town then
          there is a list of things that we
          need.

                                        CUT TO:

EXT. SIDE OF THE WAKEFIELD HOUSE. DAY.

John examines a bicycle resting against the wall.

                                        CUT TO:

INT. DINING ROOM. DAY.

Jennie sweeps the floor.

Charlotte cleans the dining room table.

                                        CUT TO:

EXT. DRY LAKE BED. DAY.

John bicycles over the dry lake bed, a small
speck against a backdrop of mountain.

The wheels spin, giving of a **metallic** buzz.

                                        CUT TO:

INT. SITTING ROOM. DAY.

Jennie brushes the curtains with a duster. Her
foot kicks a large box at the base of the window.

Jennie looks down at it.

                    JENNIE
                 (to Charlotte)
            Can you help me?

They attempt to move the box.

                    CHARLOTTE
            It's not moving at all.

                                        CUT TO:

EXT. ROAD. DAY.

John turns into the forest.

A solitary road.

                                        CUT TO:

INT. WAKEFIELD HOUSE. DAY.

Jennie leans down and opens the lid.

Both sisters look at the contents.

                    JENNIE
            It's dirt.

Charlotte leans down and sifts her hand through it.

                    JENNIE (cont'd)
          Just dirt.

Jennie leans the lid against the wall. She kneels down and puts both hands through it.

                    CHARLOTTE
          Why?

Jennie shakes her head in bewilderment.

                    JENNIE
          I don't know.

                                        CUT TO:

INT. FOREST GROVE. DAY.

John stops the bicycle. He's tired and sweating. Suddenly, he spots something around the bend of the path.

(Aric Cushing as John Weiland)

Movement.

John walks the bike towards it.

JOHN POV

Of the road up ahead. In the distance, a man stands on the side of the road with a wheel- barrow. John cannot make out the scene.

The noon day sun melts the air.

John squints.

Continues on.

Finally, John comes up to the man. A strange WOMAN stands next to him.

ANGLE ON

the MAN on the side of the road, and the woman. The man shovels rats out of a wheelbarrow and into a large pit. As John approaches, he stops.

The WOMAN looks up and moves her parasol back slightly to view John.

                    WOMAN
          You're the new doctor.

A waft of burning smoke rises up from the rat pit.

                    JOHN
          Yes. Weiland. John Weiland.

                    WOMAN
          Living at the Wakefield house?

John nods.

> WOMAN (CONT'D)
> We've always had a problem with rats
> in this town. How do you find the
> house?

> JOHN
> It's fine. Thank you.

John smiles at her.

> WOMAN
> And your wife?

> JOHN
> My wife?

> WOMAN
> Yes, your wife. And her sister too.
> Are they getting along fine?

> JOHN
> Yes, they are. We're all getting along
> just fine, thank you.

The man pitches a shovel full of rats into the
pit.

> WOMAN
> Perhaps they could come into town. We
> have a women's club there.

> JOHN
> I'll mention it to them.

> WOMAN
> Please.

                    JOHN
          Forgive me, but I have to be getting
          on now. Good day to you.

                    WOMAN
          Good day.

John gets on his bicycle and continues on.

                                        CUT TO:

CLOSE UP
of John, bicycling. He looks over his shoulder to
glance once more at the strange picture: old
herald and man with vermin.

                                        CUT TO:

EXT. TREACHEROUS MOUNTAINS. DAY.

Jennie and Charlotte walk together along a rocky
path.

                    CHARLOTTE
          How long do you think you'll stay now?

                    JENNIE
          However long you—

                    CHARLOTTE
          You don't need to stay because of me.

                    JENNIE
               (firm)
          Charlotte.

                    CHARLOTTE
          And you don't need to stay here for
          John either.

Jennie stops and reaches into her pocket.

> JENNIE
> Listen. I've been waiting to give you
> this. I found it in my pocket, the day
> after.

She hands Charlotte a tiny child's toy. Jennie
puts her hand up to her mouth.

Charlotte takes it in her hand. It is a small
thing against the barren desert around them.

> CHARLOTTE
> It's so strange that it can be so
> close to me and I can suddenly feel
> nothing.

Jennie begins to cry.

CUT TO:

INT. WAKEFIELD HOUSE. DAY.

The front door opens. John enters with a plain
brown bag of food.

Silence.

John closes the door behind him.

Suddenly there is the sound of tiny feet. A
child's feet. In the sitting room.

John immediately turns and steps into the room.

CUT TO:

INT. SITTING ROOM. DAY.

The sofa is in the center of the room surrounded by palms and various chairs. Much like the library, it is a strange museum. Deep long shadows fall from the tall windows.

                    JOHN
          Charlotte?

The sitting room is silent.

John moves into the hallway.

Empty.

At the end of the hall, John notices the door to the side porch is open.

John moves down the hall to the door. He moves through it to the small porch.

The storage room door is cracked open.

                              CUT TO:

INT. STORAGE ROOM. DAY.

John opens the door.

Charlotte is inside going through large boxes of clothes. She glances to him, but says nothing. She continues to hold up the items and examine them.

                    JOHN
          Did Jennie just come back through this
          hall?

                    CHARLOTTE
          No. She's out back starting her
          garden.

                    JOHN
          She's wasting her time. Hendricks said
          the land is useless. Nothing will
          grow.

                    CHARLOTTE
          There are trunks full of old clothing
          in here. Maybe some thigns we can use.
          . . so uch of it is rotted to dust
          (beat) What a shame.

John stands in the doorway. He says nothing for a
time.

                    JOHN
          You should not be exerting yourself.

Charlotte ignores him and continues looking at
the clothes.

John watches her sadly--and slightly angry--then
turns. . . and exits the doorway.

                                        CUT TO:

EXT. PORCH. NIGHT.

WE PAN ACROSS THE DECK

Jennie wrestles with a large black hoop dress on
her lap. She attempts to pull out the wires from
the dress. Charlotte sits next to her.

                    CHARLOTTE
          It's so quiet out here.

                    JENNIE
        Yes, strange for this time of year.

                    JENNIE (cont'd)
        Usually this kind of heat attracts so
        many bugs.

                    JOHN
        Oh.

John gets up and exits into the house.

                    JENNIE
        I don't think I can pull these out.
        They are sewn in to tightly.

Charlotte takes the dress from Jennie and starts
to look at it herself.

John comes back onto the porch.

                    JOHN
        Look at this. Look at this.

John hands Jennie a parchment. Jennie takes it
and examines the writing.

                    JENNIE
        Me?

                    JOHN
        Yes.

John hands Jennie a parchment. Jennie takes it
and examines the writing.

                    JOHN (CONT'D)
        You studied French.

                    JENNIE
Ages ago.

                    JOHN
I found it tucked away in the library.
I thought you might know what it says.

                    JENNIE
Ugh. (beat) It's a lease. From.   .   .
1785. I think.

                    JOHN
The date I can make out myself.

                    CHARLOTTE
John.

                    JENNIE
A small .   .   . in Toulouse. The rest
is just. .   . legal. To tell you the
truth, it's rather hard to read.

Jennie hands the paper back to John. John takes
it and begins to examine it himself. He moves to
the edge of the porch.

                    CHARLOTTE
Well, I suppose we'll just have to
make do with these, wear them as is.

                    JENNIE
I wish that we could forage enough
material in that house to make
something. . . (to John) More
modern.

                    CHARLOTTE
Oh, but John. We did find a coat for
you, but it's a bit worn.

Jennie holds the dress at arm's length.

              JENNIE
      This is the kind of dress Mother would
      have worn. . . every day of her
      life. What would she have done with
      it?

             CHARLOTTE
      Turned it inside out and used it as
      two dresses.

They laugh.

             JENNIE
      I think so.

             CHARLOTTE
        (automatic-forgetting)
      Sarah?

John freezes.

Jennie stops what she is doing and reaches her
hands out to her sister.

Charlotte is instantly broken - stunned.

Their silence is interrupted by a piercing

HOWL.

Everyone freezes.

Then another wild dog howls.

And another.

And another.

John stares into the vast darkness. The sounds
are coming from all around them.
Jennie and Charlotte stand up, alarmed.

John steps back from the top step of the porch.

> JOHN
> (to himself)
> I think we should go inside now.

CUT TO:

INT. JOHN AND CHARLOTTE'S ROOM. NIGHT. LATER.

Charlotte sits up in bed. Awake.

John sleeps beside her.

Charlotte pulls the covers away from her and
quietly gets out of bed.

CUT TO:

NT. SEWING ROOM. NIGHT.

Charlotte closes the bedroom door and turns to
the small door which leads up to the yellow
wallpaper room.

She turns the key, opens it.

Charlotte lifts the lantern.

The stairs are illuminated.

Charlotte disappears through the door, and up the
steps.

                                        CUT TO:

INT. JOHN AND CHARLOTTE'S ROOM. NIGHT.

John struggles with the blanket. He pulls it
slightly towards him.

The blanket pulls in the opposite direction. Half
asleep, he pulls again.

The covers slide quickly.

John turns over.

The bed is empty.

Groggy, he falls back asleep.

                                        CUT TO:

INT. THE YELLOW WALLPAPER ROOM. NIGHT.

Charlotte's lantern illuminates the room as she
moves up the staircase. It is a strange and empty
space. A rusted, metal bed. A single ornate desk.

The patterns of the wallpaper stretch in the
flickering light of the flame.

Charlotte moves to the small desk and looks down
to the scattered papers and an old ink well.

She backs up to the wall and leans against it, a
curious expression covering her face.

                    JENNIE (O.C.)
          There is something there. Behind.

                                        CUT TO:

28

EXT. UNDER THE HOUSE. DAY.

John is underneath the porch, searching. He crawls around the brick piling that holds up the old structure. John struggles through a plot of bramble.

> JENNIE
> Do you see anything?

> JOHN
> No.

He crawls into the darkest corner beneath the house.

He falters—

> JOHN
> Ugh.

Steadying himself, he squints to see a deep, wide gap in the earth.

Vines and tendrils wrap around the mouth and disappear into the pit.

> JENNIE
> What is it?

> JOHN
> A well?

> JENNIE
> What?

John leans in to hear a singing sound ringing from deep inside the raw hole.

                    JENNIE (CONT'D)
              John? What? What did you say?

John leans over and puts his hand down on a
SLIPPERY dead rat. He jerks back and up!

BANG.

John whacks his head on the rafters.

John scurries out of the crawl space. He
immediately goes to the grass and begins to wipe
off his hand. He turns and sees a pail of water
Jennie was washing the windows with. He walks to
it and sinks his hands inside.

                    JENNIE (CONT'D)
              Are you all right? What happened?

                    JOHN
              There are rats all right.

                    JENNIE
              I knew I heard something last night.
              I'll set out the traps then. We don't
              want them getting into the house.

John glances up to the window of the yellow
wallpaper room.

Charlotte moves past the window and vanishes into
the recesses of the room.

                                        CUT TO:

EXT. FRONT OF WAKEFIELD HOUSE. DAY.

A YOUNG MAN, a messenger, runs towards the house.
He reaches the front door and knocks.

Charlotte opens the door.

The young man stands before her, flushed, excited.

> CHARLOTTE
> Yes?

> YOUNG MAN
> Is the doctor here?

CUT TO:

EXT. STRETCH OF LAND. DAY.

John stands and watches the men. Everything is silent. If John's expression were a voice, it would say, 'I can't believe it's come down to this'.

(Director Logan Thomas, Ted Manson, and Alex Schemmer)

The two men stand across from each other, guns held up beside their faces. The DUEL is about to begin.

The younger of the two duellists is PETER WARE.
His expression is betrayed by his uncontrollable
shaking. DAVID KILBOURNE, the older of the two,
is serene, steady, even cocky.

(Keller Wortham as David Kilbourne)

An OLD MAN stands close to John.

                        OLD MAN
            One, two, three, four, five.

A **gunshot**.

                                        CUT TO:

John sews up DAVID KILBOURNE. Young Peter is
gushing with pride and relief.

                        JOHN
            You know this is illegal. Not to
            mention stupid.

                        OLD MAN
            Not out here son.

The needle goes in to David's arm, up and down.

                                        CUT TO:

INT. SITTING ROOM. DAY.

ANGLE ON

a needle going up and down. Jennie sits at the
sewing machine, altering an old shirt.

                                        CUT TO:

EXT. STRETCH OF LAND. DAY.

                        DAVID
            Stupid. This coming from a man who
            just moved into the Wakefields. . .
            I would look hard first before
            casting stones Doctor. . .

                    JOHN
I'd look hard first before taunting a
man who is pushing a needle into your
arm.

                    PETER
Then you like the house, Dr. Weiland?

Peter Ware stares at John from the distance.

(Alex Schemmer as Peter Ware)

The men laugh at their inside joke.

> DAVID
> Find it cozy, do you?

John, more unsettled than before, looks to them, confused.

He stops mending the arm.

> OLD MAN
> Quiet yourselves, you stupid fools.

> JOHN
> (to Peter)
> What do you mean by that sir?

> OLD MAN
> Nothing. They mean nothing.

> DAVID
> Pardon me, but I'm still bleeding.

John goes back to sewing the man.

> CUT TO:

INT. SEWING ROOM. DAY.

ANGLE ON

Jennie's back. We pull in to her as she continues to sew. She swats something at the back of her neck. After a minute, she does it again.

Jennie stops.

She turns around.

Jennie CLOSE UP

as she stares forward, trying to see if something is there.

                                        CUT TO:

INT. THE YELLOW WALLPAPER ROOM. DAY.

Charlotte writes at a small writing desk. We can hear the scrawl of her fountain pen.

Sweat beads on her forehead. Slowly she wipes it away.

After a moment, Charlotte undoes the top of her dress. And pulls it away from her. It is an erotic movement.

She drops the upper portion of her dress to the floor. The white undergarment is drenched in sweat.

                                        CUT TO:

INT. SECOND HALLWAY. DAY. LATER.

Jennie moves down the hallway towards the library.

She goes to the door and opens it.

She enters.

                                        CUT TO:

INT. LIBRARY. DAY.

John is showing Dr. Jack Everland a book.

DR. EVERLAND leans on John's desk. John stands beside him. The doctor is about fifty to sixty

years old. He has long sideburns, a nicely
trimmed mustache, and wears an impeccably
tailored brown flannel suit. He is a symbol of
the old world: rich, and over-adorned.

              JENNIE
        Excuse me. (beat) Doctor Everland?
        Would you like some tea?

            DR. EVERLAND
        That would be wonderful.

              JENNIE
        John?

              JOHN
        Yes, thank you Jennie.

Jennie nods and exits.

            DR. EVERLAND
        Yes, I think you have discovered a
        king's ransom here with these books.

Dr. Everland closes the book that John was
showing him.

              JOHN
        Well, they're not mine.

            DR. EVERLAND
        Nevertheless, I think they are
        splendid.

              JOHN
        I wish you could stay longer Jack; we
        have plenty of room.

                    DR. EVERLAND
          Thank you, but I have to be off again
          this evening. I was simply passing
          near enough to make a stop, see how
          you were doing.

                    JOHN
          I'm glad you did.

                    DR. EVERLAND
          So am I.

He sets the book down.

                    DR. EVERLAND (cont'd)
          You know John, you do not look well. I
          was wondering if you knew that.

                    JOHN
          How do you mean?

                    DR. EVERLAND
          You look tired, and so do the women.

                    JOHN
          As you can imagine, we have not
          exactly been eating or sleeping well.

                    DR. EVERLAND
          You've all had a great deal of
          misfortune.

John moves to the other side of the room.

                    DR. EVERLAND (cont'd)
          Is there anything that I can do?

                    JOHN
          No, no Jack, you've done enough.

John walks around the desk, crosses his arms, and looks out the window.

Dr. Everland says nothing. He simply watches John.

> DR. EVERLAND
> John? . . .

John turns to him.

> DR. EVERLAND (cont'd)
> I may have been your professor ten years ago, but I've been your friend for almost as long. Tell me what is on your mind?

There is a long silence.

> JOHN
> We were together... behind the house when the fire broke out.

The doctor waits.

> JOHN (CONT'D)
> Jennie was gone. It was early evening. When we got back, I ran through the front door. Everything was in flames, but. . . I ran upstairs. I couldn't help her; my baby was on fire... I couldn't reach her, Jack. I swear to God, I couldn't reach her.

John turns and looks at Dr. Everland.

> DR. EVERLAND
> I am sorry son.

                        JOHN
          I do not even know how it began. I
          didn't know--

                        DR. EVERLAND
          And how is Charlotte coping with this?

                                        CUT TO:

INT. JOHN AND CHARLOTTE'S ROOM. DAY.

CLOSE UP

of Charlotte. She sits and stares out the window.

                        JOHN O.C.
          I have known Charlotte since we were
          children, and there wasn't a moment of
          my life that I did not know I would
          spend the rest of my life with her,
          because she was so filled with life.
          Now everything I thought I knew I do
          not understand. (beat) And I do not
          understand her.

                                        CUT TO:

INT. LIBRARY. DAY.

EXTREME CLOSE UP

of Dr. Everland. His face is shrouded in shadow,
only his profile is illuminated. He is the sage
of a dream. . . whispering.

                        DR. EVERLAND
          Yes you do.

                                        CUT TO:

INT. SITTING ROOM. NIGHT.

Dr. Everland sips his tea in the sitting room.
Charlotte and Jennie sit together on a tiny old
sofa. John is seated in an overstuffed chair.

All three of them are attentive, and quiet.

                    JENNIE
               (to Dr. Everland)
          You are traveling on to San Francisco
          then?

                    DR. EVERLAND
          Yes, yes. One of my sons has a
          practice there. Have you been to the
          coast?

                    CHARLOTTE
          No, we decided not to go that far.

                    JOHN
          Smaller towns make for less doctors.

Long, terrible pause.

                    DR. EVERLAND
          Hm. And now you are here.

Dr. Everland thoughtfully puts down his tea. The
tinkle of the teacup sounds as the saucer is
placed on the table.

                    JENNIE
          Doctor, how is your mother?

                    DR. EVERLAND
          Half a year past ninety and no end in
          sight.

Polite smiles from John, Charlotte and Jennie.

Silence.

                DR. EVERLAND (cont'd)
        And you are well, Charlotte?

Taken aback.

                CHARLOTTE
        Yes, fine, thank you.

                DR. EVERLAND
        You know, it's not too late to have
        another baby.

                JOHN
        Jack--

                DR. EVERLAND
        Never underestimate a woman's need to
        have a child John. It overrides all
        other priorities. It makes her spirit
        whole.

The women attempt to hide expressions of horror.

Dr. Everland beams a warm smile at the educated,
fatherly advice that he has given to the family.

                DR. EVERLAND (cont'd)
            (to Charlotte)
        After all my dear, what else does a
        woman have, if not the joy of
        creation.

                                CUT TO:

INT. JENNIE'S ROOM. NIGHT.

Jennie splashes water on her face. Charlotte sits
on the bed.

                    JENNIE
          How dare he. To suggest such a thing.
          A child so soon. It's brash. He is
          too... European.

                    CHARLOTTE
          He's only saying what he thinks will
          help.

                    JENNIE
          Psst. He's only saying what a man
          would think would help.

                    CHARLOTTE
               (beat)
          He is only a man.

                                        CUT TO:

INT. ENTRYWAY. NIGHT.

Dr. Everland is ready to leave. John stands with
him in the entryway.

                    JOHN
          Jack. Please consider staying the
          night.

                    DR. EVERLAND
          If I could afford the time. . .

                    JOHN
          I wish that I could understand why you
          have to be there so quickly. Can you
          not spare one more day?

                    DR. EVERLAND
          Christopher has syphilis. He is dying.

                    JOHN
                    (saddened)
          Oh no.

                    DR. EVERLAND
          He's only just begun his practice. In
          some terrible way I think I have
          actually come to you for advice.
          (beat) I've never lost a child John. I
          know he is a man now, but all I keep
          seeing is my little boy, and there is
          nothing that I can do. (a little
          smirk) Physician--

Dr. Everland puts on his coat.

                    DR. EVERLAND (CONT'D)
          Well.   . . we stand at the cusp of
          the abyss, my boy.

                    JOHN
          You have my prayers.

                    DR. EVERLAND
          We'll need them.

                                        CUT TO:

INT. JOHN AND CHARLOTTE'S ROOM. NIGHT.

John wakes up as if from a nightmare. He looks
over to the other side of the bed. Charlotte is
gone.

John gets up from the bed. He moves toward the bedroom door and opens it and listens. Silence.

                                    CUT TO:

INT. SITTING ROOM. NIGHT.

John moves into the sitting room. All the windows are open. John rubs his arms.

                    JOHN
          Charlotte?

Nothing.

John walks to the first window. He glances outside before sliding it shut. He turns and goes to the next window and does the same.

John turns back to go to his room.

A WITHERED OLD BLACK MAN stands at the center of the room. Expression, impassive. Eyes, wide and still.

John freezes.

Wind howls through the last open window.

                    JOHN (cont'd)
                    (panicked)
          What are you doing in here? Who are
          you!? Answer me!

The man does not move, nor respond.

After a moment, the man turns and exits into the hall.

John follows him quickly.

CUT TO:

INT. FIRST HALLWAY. NIGHT.

John enters the hallway.

The man is gone.

John rushes to the second hallway.

Empty.

He moves down it quickly.

John turns into the storage room and runs into
Charlotte.

> JOHN
> (angry)
> Did you just see a man in here?

> CHARLOTTE
> What? No.

> JOHN
> There's someone in the house.

CUT TO:

INT. JENNIE'S ROOM. NIGHT.

John bursts into her room, pulling Charlotte.

> JENNIE
> (jerking up)
> What is it?

> JOHN
> Lock the door.

John runs out of the room.

                                        CUT TO:

INT. JENNIE'S ROOM. NIGHT.

Charlotte quickly closes the door and locks it.

                    JENNIE
          What's happening?

                                        CUT TO:

INT. ENTRYWAY. NIGHT.

John stumbles into the entryway.

He stands still and listens.

Looks around nervously.

John moves to the sliding wooden doors to the
dining room. He throws them open.

Moonlight glints off the large table at the
center of the room.

John fumbles to the sideboard.

Without taking his eyes from the room, he reaches
for the lantern. He shakes it.

Empty.

John's hand grapples over the front of the
sideboard and opens the silverware drawer.
He pulls out a spoon.

Throws it down.

Finds a knife.

                                    CUT TO:

He snatches up a box of matches.

Leans over to the candelabra in the center of the
table.

Frantically tries to light the old candles.

Looks over his shoulder.

He shakes badly.

His frustration rises at how long it takes to
light them.

Finishes.

John holds up the candelabra and points it out in
front of him.

                                    CUT TO:

INT. LIBRARY. NIGHT.

The door creaks open.

John enters the library.

He moves across the room.

Peers around the desk.

Nothing.

He turns--

Into--

a stuffed, open mouthed SNAKE.

John jumps.

Relieved, he begins to turn and exit the library.

The candles barely illuminate the strange
crevices of the room.

As he moves towards the door WE SEE a gaunt, open
eyed EIGHTEENTH CENTURY WOMAN clutching the wall.

Only for a moment. She's as sickly pale as her
faded dress.

John does not see her.

He exits.

CUT TO:

INT. JENNIE'S ROOM. NIGHT.

A knock at the door.

> JOHN O.C.
> Charlotte?

> CHARLOTTE
> John?

> JOHN O.C.
Stay in there. I have to check one more room.

CUT TO:

INT. SEWING ROOM. NIGHT.

John moves into the sewing room. He holds up the candelabra.

Empty.

BANG.

John jerks, then turns towards the door to the yellow wallpaper room.

Another BANG coming from the yellow wallpaper room.

John goes to the door.

It opens with a gust of air.

John raises the candelabra.

                                        CUT TO:

INT. THE YELLOW WALLPAPER ROOM. NIGHT.

John reaches the top of the stairs.

It is the first time he has actually stepped into the room.

A strange breathing out sounds in the emptiness.

A single shutter bangs against an open window.

John closes it.

Turns.

A metal bed sits in the dim light at the end of the room.

The patterns of the wallpaper dance in the candlelight.

                                    DISSOLVE TO:

INT. DINING ROOM. NEXT MORNING.

White morning light fills the house.

John leans against the sideboard. Jennie and Charlotte stand across from him. Both of the women stand separate, arms crossed, same expression, mirrors of each other.

                    CHARLOTTE
                    (exhausted)
          Perhaps he was a previous tenant. And
          he came back for something. Or left
          something here.

                    JOHN
          That doesn't make any sense. I told
          you. His manner was cold. He did not
          look like he was searching for
          anything at all.

John tips a suspicious brow at Charlotte.

                    CHARLOTTE
          I don't know.

                    JENNIE
          This could be my fault. I should have
          thought to lock up the house.

                    CHARLOTTE
                    (to Jennie)
          We've never kept the doors locked
          before. I don't want to start now.

                    JOHN
        We don't know anyone here. Jennie is
        right. We keep the doors locked.

Suddenly, a woman's voice can be heard in the
distance.

All three of them cock their heads.

Jennie moves to the window.

Jennie POV

an entourage of ladies moving towards the house,
decked out and plumed.

                    JENNIE O.C.
        Oh no.

John and Charlotte nestle beside Jennie, to look.

                    JOHN
        What is it?

The women's bright dresses blow around them as
they cackle.

                    JENNIE O.C.
        By all accounts. . . a flock of
        chickens.

                                        CUT TO:

EXT. FRONT PORCH. DAY.

Four WOMEN move over the porch in the blazing hot
white sun. Their dresses shudder in the wind and
the dust rises up around them. They hold their
parasols above their heads to protect them from

the heat. It is a strange party.

The front door opens.

MRS. DAYGERON is a fifty five year old, dainty woman. She is dressed impeccably and has wise features.

MRS. TREMAYNE is a thirty something porcelain doll.

MRS. STEELE is a forty year old woman, large and jolly.

MRS. FOUCOULT is twenty eight, with blonde wavy hair. She is disheveled, in an irritating way.

>   MRS. STEELE
>   (huge smile)
>   Hello my dears. Welcome.

>   CUT TO:

INT. SITTING ROOM. DAY.

SINGLE SHOT
of Charlotte sitting in a chair. Her black dress flows out around her.

Jennie sits beside her.

The women are scattered around the room in a loose semi-circle of chairs and sofas. Multiple conversations occur at the same time, a wild little chatter.

>   MRS. STEELE
>   (to Mrs. Daygeron)
>   I've always wanted to come. My
>   husband, Peter, would never allow

                    MRS. STEELE (CONT'D
          it...

                    MRS. TREMAYNE
                      (to Jennie)
          Oh dear. There is a dress shop right
          in town, and I can loan you something
          for the time being...

                    JENNIE
          I fear the outcome.

Close on Mrs. Daygeron.

                    MRS. DAYGERON
                      (to Mrs. Foucoult)
          Terrifying...

Mrs. Steele is clutching her tea cup.

                    MRS. FOUCOULT
                      (to Charlotte)
          ...and Mr. Temil confessed that one of
          his dogs had gotten hold of his wife's
          prized pheasant, and run off.

Charlotte grins halfheartedly.

                    CHARLOTTE
                      (to Mrs. Steele)
          Really?

                    MRS. FOUCOULT
          Why, the two of you don't even look
          like sisters.

Jennie stands.

Everyone looks up at her.

                    JENNIE
                (to everyone)
        Ladies, please excuse me.

Jennie exits.

Mrs. Tremayne begins whispering to Mrs. Foucoult.
Mrs. Steele turns back to Charlotte, flashes a
big awkward smile and shrugs.

                                        CUT TO:

INT. LIBRARY. DAY.

John walks across the room and sits on the edge
of his desk.

                                        CUT TO:

INT. SITTING ROOM. DAY.

Mrs. Tremayne and Mrs. Foucoult sit together.

                    MRS. TREMAYNE
                (to Mrs. Foucoult)
        . . . could get them another
            house.

                    MRS. FOUCOULT
                (to Mrs. Tremayne)
            Shssh.

The tide of chatter rises and falls.

                                        CUT TO:

INT. LIBRARY. DAY.

John loads a rifle. He holds it up and checks it
against the light from the window.

                                        CUT TO:

INT. SITTING ROOM. DAY.

Close of Charlotte.

Her large eyes stare forward as the walls seem to
fall away.

The voices in the room have become a chorus of
murmurs.

She is lost... watching tiny bits of dust float
through a long sodium shaft of sunlight.

The noise seems to close in.

The conversation, deeper and louder.

Until-

                    CHARLOTTE
                 (to everyone)
            Ladies, would you please excuse me for
            a moment.

                                        CUT TO:

INT. KITCHEN. DAY.

Jennie stands in the kitchen. She sips her tea.
Alone. Reflective.

Charlotte enters.

                    CHARLOTTE
            What do you think of our guests?

                    JENNIE
What do you think I think of our
guests?

                    CHARLOTTE
I know what you think.

                    JENNIE
These are the very type of women I've
spent my life attempting to separate
myself from. They do not have a clue
of what is going on in the world right
now.

                    CHARLOTTE
Maybe they do not wish to know.

                    JENNIE
They choose not to know. (beat) They
live in a time capsule.

                    CHARLOTTE
          (motioning to her dress)
They may live in it, but we look it.
Perhaps we'll start a trend.

                    JENNIE
          (raised voice)
No.

                    CHARLOTTE
          (slightly laughing)
They are going to hear us.

                    JENNIE
I care not.

They laugh, two innocent sisters.

Charlotte falls quiet and watches Jennie.

                    JENNIE (CONT'D)
Charlotte, I've been thinking. I want
to go back East. I feel that you and
John need to be alone right now.

                    CHARLOTTE
          (surprised)
No.

                    JENNIE
I came out here to help you with the
baby, but now. . . You are going to
be just fine. I don't think you need
me here anymore.

                    CHARLOTTE
          (stopping her)
I can't survive what's happening
alone.

                    JENNIE
You are not alone, Charlotte.

                    CHARLOTTE
Aren't I?

                    MRS. DAYGERON
          (from the other room, singing)
Ladies! We'll begin to talk about you
if you do not come out soon.

                    JENNIE
          (ignoring)
Charlotte. I've reached an age where
I've become a woman of no means. Or
position. And the chances of my
marrying now are slim. No amount of
education can change that. When Sarah
was alive, it was easy to forget these

                    JENNIE (CONT'D)
things. (beat) I traded my security
for knowledge, and those qualities are
not exactly considered desirable in a
woman. Now, when I see you and John
together, it only reminds me of...what
I will not have in my life.

                    CHARLOTTE
What know you of John and me?

                    JENNIE
John is a good man for you. You have
to let him be a good man for you.
(beat) You love him.

                    CHARLOTTE
I...yes...I mean, I don't remember.

                    JENNIE
What are you saying?

                    CHARLOTTE
I can't remember anything. . . I can
remember it with my mind. But not my
heart. (long beat) Please . . . I
need you to stay here with us. With
me.

                                    CUT TO:

INT. DINING ROOM. NIGHT.

John sits at the table, eating.

                    JOHN
Where is Jennie?

                    CHARLOTTE
She wasn't hungry.

John drinks from his glass.

                 JOHN
Where were you last night? (beat) I
woke up, and you were gone.

                 CHARLOTTE
I couldn't sleep.

                 JOHN
Strange that you did not wake me.

                 CHARLOTTE
I couldn't sleep. I went into one of
the spare rooms to write.

                 JOHN
The attic?

                 CHARLOTTE
Yes.

                 JOHN
To write.

                 CHARLOTTE
I just told you that.

                 JOHN
You blame me for what happened.

Charlotte stares at her husband in shock.

Jennie BURSTS into the room.

                 JENNIE
There is someone on the roof!

John stares at her for a minute, confused.

                        JENNIE (cont'd)
                          (frantic)
          The roof! Something is on the roof!
          John gets up, confused, immediately
          reacting. He moves into the hallway.

                        CHARLOTTE
          John.

          He heads toward the library with the women
          following him.

                        CHARLOTTE (CONT'D)
          You're not going to go out there? It
          could be the man from the other night.

                        JOHN
          It's most likely nothing at all. It's
          probably the rats.

                        JENNIE
          Rats? What I heard was not a rat.

                        JOHN
          Jennie. You always overreact.

                        JENNIE
          I do not overreact, John.

                        CHARLOTTE
          Please.

                        JENNIE (CONT'D)
                          (to Charlotte)
          Please what? Be quiet?

                        JOHN
                          (to Jennie)
          You always make up stories.

                    CHARLOTTE
          John. Stop antagonizing her.

                    JOHN
                (to Charlotte)
          I haven't even begun to antagonize
          her—

BOOM!

Everyone jumps.

Both women move to the walls.

Thundering footsteps tromp across the roof.

John freezes in the center of the hall.

                    JENNIE
                (looking dead at John)
          Big rats.

                                        CUT TO:

EXT. PORCH. NIGHT.

John moves down the front steps of the house with
a lantern and the rifle from the library.

                                        CUT TO:

EXT. SIDE OF THE HOUSE. NIGHT.

He steps along the side of the house.

Looks up to the roof.

Nothing.

John hears something and turns.

Behind him, in the blackness, a figure moves away from the house.

John stands still and looks forward.

ANGLE ON
Charlotte and Jennie in the sitting room. They peer out the window at him.

OVER JOHN'S SHOULDER

we see a girl child.

Running.

Under the moonlight.

She disappears in the brush.

John catches her last few steps.

STUNNED.

John stands frozen.

Then he chases the child into the tall grass.

The lantern swings wildly as he searches.

John looks up.

In the distance, the girl disappears into another hill of grass.

John chases.

He bursts through the tall weeds and turns on...
the crouched, shadowed figure of a man.

The man leaps up, frightened.

Both men rear back in shock.

John drops the lantern.

The man bolts towards the road.

John pursues.

                    JOHN
          You! Stop!

Clumsily, John fumbles through the brush with the
heavy rifle.

He trips.

The rifle tumbles into the tall grass.

John reaches franticly to find it. He sees the
man gaining distance.

John runs.

WIDE SHOT

of two tiny figures racing over a barren field.

                    JOHN
                 (yelling)
          Stop!

John catches up to the man, just barely getting
hold of his shirt.

It tears.

                    JOHN
          Wait! STOP!

The man slips.

Stumbles.

The man gives up and faces John, breathing hard. Still holding the man's shirt, John shakes him.

> JOHN
> Who are you? What were you doing? This is my house! What are you doing!?

The man is out of breath.

> MAN IN FIELD
> Please--

> JOHN
> What were you doing? Answer me!

> MAN IN FIELD
> Please, I'm just looking. I'm looking for my family--

> JOHN
> (out of breath)
> Family?

> MAN IN FIELD
> My family stayed here last winter. . . .

John lets the man go.

> MAN IN FIELD O.C.
> I haven't seen them since. I thought I could—

> JOHN
> How did you get on our roof?

           MAN IN FIELD
          (blank expression)
I wasn't on your roof. I saw you
through the window, and I knew my
family wasn't here anymore.(beat) Then
I saw someone else.

           JOHN
          (agitated again)
Who? Where? What did you see?

           MAN IN FIELD
Someone else.

           JOHN
Someone else? A child?

           MAN IN FIELD
No. I don't know. I just want to go
home now. Please, please let me go
home.

The man begins to break down.

John stands in the moonlight with a horrified
expression.

                  CUT TO:

INT. ENTRYWAY. NIGHT.

John re-enters the house. He closes the door
behind him.

           JOHN
It was a man. Looking for his family.

                    JENNIE
               (sarcastically)
          On the roof.

John is in a daze.

                    JOHN
          No, no he wasn't on our roof...
          they had stayed here ...

                    CHARLOTTE
          John, you are rambling. Where's the
          lantern and gun?

He looks at Charlotte.

                    JOHN
          What...?

She steps closer to him.

                    CHARLOTTE
          John, are you alright?

                    JENNIE
               (a little hysterical)
          So you're saying someone else was up
          there!?

                    CHARLOTTE
          John.

He looks up at her.

                    CHARLOTTE (CONT'D)
          What is it? Did you see something
          else?

The room falls silent. He shakes his head.

                         JOHN
              No, I didn't see anything else.

                         JENNIE
              John!

                         JOHN
              Everything is fine.

John exits the entryway and moves into the
hallway.

Jennie turns to Charlotte, enraged. Charlotte
returns her sister's gaze.

                                        CUT TO:

INT. THE YELLOW WALLPAPER ROOM. NIGHT.

PAN OVER

the yellow wallpaper to Charlotte. Charlotte
closes one of the windows. She locks it.

CLOSE UP

of Charlotte. She turns and looks over her
shoulder.

The wind kicks up from the one open window.
The lantern flame flickers.

Charlotte stares down the expanse of the attic
room to the metal bed and the shadows at the end
of the room.

We HOLD ON the wall and the bed.

Charlotte turns and glances out the window before
shutting it.

CHARLOTTE POV

of the house and the ground, two stories below.
A slow fog creeps over the ground.

Charlotte thoughtfully pulls herself back into
the room. She begins to close the window... and
backs into...

John.

She gives a little jump, that quickly melts into
an embarrassed smile.

                    CHARLOTTE
          Oh, John, I didn't hear you.

                    JOHN
          I'm sorry, you were gone for awhile...
          What are you looking at?

He leans past her to peer out the window.

                    CHARLOTTE
          A mist rolling in--it must mean rain.

                    JOHN
          Hmm. . . it doesn't feel like rain.

She smiles and closes the window.

                    JOHN (CONT'D)
          I'm going to bed now. Are you coming?

                    CHARLOTTE
          Yes.

                              CUT TO:

EXT. THE WAKEFIELD HOUSE. NEXT DAY.

It is a scorching day.

Heat swells over the grass.

The Wakefield house sits in the distance.

In a small clearing, John cuts wood on a chopping
block. He tries to chop each piece in half, but
he clearly looks out of place as he swings and
misses almost every time.

                              CUT TO:

EXT. WALKWAY TO WAKEFIELD HOUSE. DAY.

Charlotte moves down the front walkway. She
reaches the mailbox and places some letters
inside.

She turns back to the house.

On her walk back to the house, Charlotte glances
to an adjacent field. She sees John chopping
wood. He does not see her.

                              CUT TO:

EXT. PORCH. DAY.

Charlotte reaches the porch and moves up the
steps. She stops and turns.

CLOSE UP

of Charlotte as she leans against the porch post.
She watches John with an expression of
tenderness.

He tips his head side to side, much like a
confused puppy.

She laughs quietly to herself.

                                        CUT TO:

INT. ENTRYWAY. DAY.

Charlotte enters the house. She goes and picks up
her book off the center table.

She turns and walks back out the front door.

                                        CUT TO:

EXT. FRONT PORCH. DAY.

Charlotte moves to the wicker chair, and past the
tall windows into the sitting room.

She sits down.

In the background, through the window pane,
stands Sarah's tiny, pale figure. It is obscured
by the white lace of the shifting window curtain.

                    SARAH O.S.
                   (whispers)
          Mommy.

Charlotte jerks up, reacting instantly.

                    SARAH O.S. (CONT'D)
          Mommy.

Charlotte drops the book and stands. She sees the
misty figure of Sarah through the window.

> CHARLOTTE
Sarah!

Charlotte bursts into the house.

> CUT TO:

INT. ENTRYWAY. DAY.

Charlotte runs through the entryway and into...

> CUT TO:

INT. SITTING ROOM. DAY.

Sarah is gone.

> SARAH O.S.
> (in the distance)
Mommy.

Charlotte runs into the hallway.

> CHARLOTTE
SARAH!

> CUT TO:

EXT. CLEARING. DAY.

John jerks up, at the scream.

He throws the axe down and runs towards the house.

> CUT TO:

INT. SECOND HALLWAY. DAY.

Charlotte rushes through the hallway to the

sewing room.

                                        CUT TO:

INT. SEWING ROOM. DAY.

Charlotte grabs the door to the yellow wallpaper
room and throws it open.

                    CHARLOTTE

        Sarah?!

                                        CUT TO:

INT. THE YELLOW WALLPAPER ROOM. DAY.

She runs up the stairs and towards the yellow
wallpaper.

                                        CUT TO:

EXT. DRY LAKE BED. DAY.

STARK HARD SAND.

Jennie's burgundy dress flaps in the wind as she rides the squeaky little bike over the dry lake bed.

Her figure is a weird apparition against the prehistoric plane.

                              CUT TO:

INT. HALLWAY. DAY.

John bursts into the hall.

                    JOHN
              Charlotte!

                              CUT TO:

INT. THE YELLOW WALLPAPER ROOM. DAY.

Charlotte scratches at the wall. She attempts to pull the wallpaper away from the wood.

John reaches the open door.

Charlotte turns.

The door slams shut.

John grabs the knob.

The door gives a little.

John can see a sliver of Charlotte, trying to open it from the other side.

Suddenly the door starts to jerk wildly.

John holds onto the handle.

For an instant, through the opening, John sees---
Another face!?

A violent SLAM sends John to the floor of the
hallway and Charlotte to the floor of the room.

Beat.

Quietly the slender door glides open.

Battered, John and Charlotte look across at each
other.

                                        CUT TO:

EXT. DIRT ROAD. DAY.

Jennie rides over the narrow dirt road.

A tiny figure moves through the trees. Jennie
catches a glimpse of it out of the corner of her
eye.

She rides closer.

Through the brush, in the glaring sun, she sees
what appears to be a burnt child. . . walking
dazed.

Jennie screams.

                                        CUT TO:

INT. SITTING ROOM. DAY.

                    JENNIE
          I know what I saw.

Jennie holds a cloth to her scratched arm.
Charlotte sits on the sofa, staring forward.

John paces.

> JOHN
> How?

> JENNIE
> (softly)
> Does there need to be a reason?

> CHARLOTTE
> I heard a voice. A child's voice. (to
> John) Now you'd said you'd seen a
> girl--

> JENNIE
> What?!

> CHARLOTTE
> Last night, outside, John thought he'd
> seen the figure of a little girl.

> JENNIE
> (to John)
> John?

John is silent.

> JENNIE (CONT'D)
> Well then, we have to leave here as
> soon as possible.

> JOHN
> Where do you suggest that we go?

> JENNIE
> Anywhere, back East, stay with your
> father.

Charlotte looks at John.

                    JOHN
You know that's not an option for me.

                    JENNIE
Staying here could be dangerous.

                    CHARLOTTE
We don't know that.

                    JENNIE
               (to John)
What do we do?

                    JOHN
Tomorrow I'll go into town. I'll speak
with Mr. Hendricks, see if he has
something else, another house.

                    JENNIE
I don't trust Mr. Hendricks.
Charlotte looks over to Jennie.

                    CHARLOTTE
Why?

                    JENNIE
It's just all too strange. This house.
The way he inquired about us after the
fire. . . This place is filled with
other people's belongings. I mean
truly, how would he even know about
us?

                    CHARLOTTE
By virtue of his vocation I would
guess.

                    JENNIE
That far away? And now this!

She motions to her scratched arm.

> JOHN
> All right. Enough. (beat) The two of
> you begin writing inquiries for
> another home, and I will deal with Mr.
> Hendricks. We are educated, civilized
> people. We will not let this get the
> better of us. (beat). . . give in
> to fear and panic. We must go on as
> normal. We will behave as though
> nothing has even happened.

CUT TO:

INT. SITTING ROOM. SAME DAY.

John, Charlotte, and Jennie sit close on two
sofas. The enormous room seems to envelope them.
They are silent--uncomfortable.

> JOHN
> (to Jennie)
> Could you hand me that book, please?

Jennie looks over to the side table by the sofa.
Charlotte follows her gaze to the table, then
reaches over and picks up John's book. She passes
it to Jennie, who passes it to John.

John takes the book. Before looking down at the
book, John looks up and around the room.

CUT TO:

INT. JOHN AND CHARLOTTE'S ROOM. NIGHT.

Charlotte closes the bedroom window.

John enters.

                    JOHN
          I told Jennie to lock her door. I told
          her to call out. . . if anything at
          all happens.

Charlotte looks at her husband.

                    CHARLOTTE
          John.

                    JOHN
          Uhmm?

                    CHARLOTTE
          Has it occurred to you that Sarah is
          here? With us.

John turns to her.

                    JOHN
          Yes. It has... You weren't expecting
          that answer?

                    CHARLOTTE
          I'm not leaving here. (beat) Sarah is
          here. (beat) By some grace of God, or
          outside of God. . . I don't care.
          She is here in this house, and I am
          not going to leave her again.

                    JOHN
          Sarah is gone. Nothing that happens
          here is going to change that.

                    CHARLOTTE
          That is the doctor talking, not my
          husband.

                    JOHN
          Facts, Charlotte, are not a matter of
          intelligence or emotion, they're
          simply facts.

John looks at her.

                    CHARLOTTE
          For the first time since that night I
          feel hope, here. We can't leave until
          we at least try to understand this.
          (beat) Opportunity. For us both.

                                        CUT TO:

INT. DREAM SEQUENCE.

Sunlight blasts towards us. It is blinding.

A small girl walks through the grass, a toddler,
a cherub. She turns into camera, and claps her
chubby hands.

                    SARAH
          I love you Papa!

JOHN POV

as Sarah looks up and towards him.

                                        CUT TO:

INT. THE YELLOW WALLPAPER ROOM. DAY.

John awakes. Tears stream down his face.

Disoriented, he looks around.

John shifts to the edge of the bed. His eyes are
black holes, sunken. He looks ill--exsanguinated.

Daylight streams from the window.

The lamp light glows from the floor by the bed.
John stands up. He wipes the tears from his face.

                                        CUT TO:

INT. DINING ROOM. DAY.

Charlotte moves through the room.

John enters, groggy and disoriented.

                    CHARLOTTE
          What were you doing?

                    JOHN
          What do you mean?

                    CHARLOTTE
          You left in the middle of the night.

                    JOHN
          What?

                    CHARLOTTE
          You said you were going upstairs to
          sleep.

Charlotte stares at her husband.

                    JOHN
          I did?

                    CHARLOTTE
          Yes. You said the room was too hot.
          (beat) Have you seen Jennie? I can't
          find her.

John stares out the front window.

                    CHARLOTTE (CONT'D)
          She's not in her room.

Outside, in the clearing, in the morning mist...
Stands Jennie.

                                        CUT TO:

EXT. FRONT OF WAKEFIELD HOUSE. DAY.

John and Charlotte rush down the steps. Charlotte
carries a shawl.

JOHN AND CHARLOTTE POV

of Jennie's back, as they approach.

                    CHARLOTTE
          Jennie?

(Logan directs Dale Dickey)

Jennie stands before two open graves.

She turns to them, flushed from the brisk morning
air.
At the bottom of each hole lies a coffin.

>   JENNIE
>   I dreamed it.

John glances to her, then looks back down into
the pit.

Charlotte tries to wrap Jennie in the shawl.

>   CHARLOTTE
>   (panic)
>   Have you been out here all night?
>   John begins to climb down to the
>   coffins.

>   CHARLOTTE (CONT'D)
>   John. Don't.

>   JENNIE
>   (to Charlotte)
>   There are two.

John wrestles with the top of one wooden coffin.

>   CHARLOTTE
>   (frightened)
>   John! Please.

John pulls back the lid.

>   CHARLOTTE (CONT'D)
>   John, no!

Empty.

He lets the lid fall.

> CHARLOTTE (CONT'D)
> I don't understand, who would do such
> a thing?

> JOHN
> I don't know.

Charlotte begins to turn with her arm around
Jennie.

> CHARLOTTE
> And to leave them buried here when
> here is a cemetery so close by.

> JOHN
> What are you talking about?

She stops and looks back at John.

> CHARLOTTE
> About half an acre. South of the
> house. There's a cemetery there.

John angrily looks in the direction his wife has
pointed to.

> CHARLOTTE (CONT'D)
> (to Jennie)
> Come now, let's get you inside.

Jennie looks at her hands.

Charlotte holds Jennie and tries to warm her up.
Charlotte leads Jennie away from the graves.

John remains. He goes to the pile of dirt and
picks up Jennie's discarded shovel. He looks at
it, then lets it fall.

John walks away from the graves and towards the direction Charlotte indicated.

                                        CUT TO:

INT. DINING ROOM. DAY.

Jennie and Charlotte sit at the dining room table. Charlotte washes Jennie's hands off with a rag.

                    JENNIE
          I have a vague memory--

Charlotte looks up.

                    JENNIE (CONT'D)
          Of something long and dark, with red
          eyes. Much like the sunset. Then, I
          seemed to be sinking into deep, green
          water. And there was a singing. . .
          in my ears, like the voice of the sea.
          Inviting me. . .(she looks to
          Charlotte as she pulls out of her
          trance). . . to wander. I am so
          tired.

                    CHARLOTTE
          Of course you're tired. You have been
          up all night. I'm putting you to bed.

                    JENNIE
          There is something wrong here,
          Charlotte.

                    CHARLOTTE
          Only misunderstood.

                         JENNIE
                No, something terrible.

                                          CUT TO:

EXT. HILL TO CEMETERY. DAY.

John emerges over the knoll and stops. He looks
down at the small graveyard.

ANGLE ON

the graveyard. Neglected wooden crosses drown in
the tall weeds. Wicked old trees surround the
spot with a canopy of falling leaves.

His body moves among the old graves.

He stops.

A wood marker stands, tilted.

John squints at it.

There is no engraving.

A wind blows up leaves in his direction.

Towering over him is the statue of a robed angel.
Its stone head bowed low. One finger pointed to
Heaven.

In a sudden burst of frustration, John kicks one
of the wood crosses.

Silent. He stands in the shadow of the giant
statue.

                                          CUT TO:

EXT. FRONT OF WAKEFIELD HOUSE. DAY.

Jennie puts a small bag in the back of the carriage. Charlotte and John are a few feet beyond.

Jennie turns to them.

Charlotte hugs her sister.

Jennie stares at her for a long moment.

> CHARLOTTE
> You don't have to come back you know.

> JENNIE
> Please don't say that.

John stands in the distance.

> JENNIE (CONT'D)
> Come with me.

With a sad smile, Charlotte shakes her head 'no'. Jennie hugs her sister.

> JENNIE (CONT'D)
> You will hear from me soon.

Jennie gets into the carriage. She closes the door.

Charlotte watches the carriage move off.

John walks up to her side. He takes her hand.

WE PULL BACK ON THEM

as they stand, two shadowy figures against the backdrop of the Wakefield house.

                                        CUT TO:

INT. LIBRARY. DAY.

John sifts through another drawer of his desk.
Charlotte sits on the floor, reading through old
letters.

                    CHARLOTTE
          You haven't read any of these?

                    JOHN
          It never occurred to me to do so.

                    CHARLOTTE
          What are we looking for?

                    JOHN
          Any kind of information to this house
          or anyone who's stayed here before us.
          You're a writer, you know what to look
          for.

Charlotte sits on the floor in an ocean of aged
papers.

                                        CUT TO:

INT. LIBRARY. NIGHT. LATER.

Charlotte turns to the first page of a journal.

                    CHARLOTTE
          1862.

                    JOHN
          The war?

                    CHARLOTTE
          Yes.

                    JOHN
          Long time ago.

                    CHARLOTTE
          Dear brother Marshal. . . (skipping
          down) We are waiting for word of Jack,
          and do not know what is happening in
          Pennsylvania.

                                        CUT TO:

A MONTAGE OF SHOTS

EXT. PORCH. DAY.

                    JOHN O.S.
          Susan is behaving strangely and
          telling us stories that are
          fantastical. She is quite a
          storyteller with her tales of the
          whisper people. She hears them in the
          walls.

Charlotte watches John as he reads.

                                        CUT TO:

EXT. FIELD. DAY.

John and Charlotte walk through a field of
flowers. The noonday heat seems to melt the air
around them as they walk and talk.

                    JOHN
          You know, what's happening here could
          be good. Maybe they come here, for
          peace... drawn to this place.

The wind whirls up around them.

                                        CUT TO:

INT. DINING ROOM. NIGHT.

Charlotte sets the table for dinner. She puts
down an oil lamp on the table and turns to the
sideboard to get the silverware. When she turns
back, the lantern is on the other side of the
table.

Charlotte looks at it.

But fear does not consume her. Instead,
wonderment--a quiet comforting satisfaction.

                                        CUT TO:

INT. THE YELLOW WALLPAPER ROOM. DAY.

John comes up behind Charlotte.

                    JOHN
          A new story?

                    CHARLOTTE
          I've been inspired.

                                        CUT TO:

EXT. FRONT OF WAKEFIELD HOUSE. DAY.

An empty chair sits in the grass.

John lies on a blanket. He looks up to Charlotte.

                    JOHN V.O.
          The front pattern does move-and no
          wonder! The woman behind shakes it.
          Sometimes I think there are a great
          many women behind, and sometimes only
          one, and she crawls around fast, and
          her crawling shakes it all over. She
          is all the time trying to climb
          through. But nobody could climb
          through that pattern-it strangles so.

She dances for him.

                                        CUT TO:

INT. JOHN AND CHARLOTTE'S ROOM. NIGHT.

John and Charlotte are dressed in their night
clothes. Both sit on opposite sides of the bed.
It is an innocent finding of two souls,
rediscovering each other.

John turns the last page of Charlotte's story.

                    JOHN
          I like it. I think. . . I think it's
          very good.

                    CHARLOTTE
          It's all right.

                    JOHN
          And who is behind the wallpaper. You?

                    CHARLOTTE
          Maybe. It doesn't really matter.

Though neither of them address it, both have
sunken eyes and gaunt faces. Pale, and somewhat
deathly. Their excitement with each other

contrasts their dead looking skin.

CUT TO:

EXT. GRAVEYARD. DAY.

ANGLE ON

a hole in the ground.

Charlotte places Sarah's toy (the one Jennie gave her earlier) in the hole. She leans down, and covers it with dirt.

The wind moves a few stray hairs across her face. She is still.

In the distance, the low roll of thunder.

CUT TO:

INT. ENTRYWAY. NIGHT.

John enters the house from the rain. He shakes off his jacket and closes the door.

Past John, Charlotte blows out the candles in the sitting room.

CUT TO:

INT. CENTER HALLWAY. NIGHT.

As Charlotte closes the interior shutters at the end of the hallway, John enters from the foyer, crosses the hall, and disappears into the bedroom.

Rain taps the windows.

Charlotte moves to the second hallway and exits.
John re-emerges in the hallway and goes to the
cabinet in the wall.

                                        CUT TO:

INT. SECOND HALLWAY. NIGHT.

Charlotte's body is dwarfed in the huge expanse
of the hall. She moves towards camera. She douses
a light, then continues on towards the library.

She passes the library door.

She does not see.

A mutilated man in the doorway! Decayed.

                                        CUT TO:

INT. FIRST HALLWAY. NIGHT.

John holds a bottle of whiskey in one hand and a
glass in the other. He blows the dust off the
bottle and examines it.

A knock at the door. Not the front door, but the
side door at the end of the hall.

John looks up and down the hall.

The rain beats against the glass.

John moves towards the door.

A little hesitant, he opens it.

John peaks out into the rain.

Nothing.

Only rain.

Slowly, he closes the door.

                    CHARLOTTE O.S.
                 (screaming)
           JOHN!

John turns and runs.

                                        CUT TO:

INT. SECOND HALLWAY. NIGHT.

Charlotte stands at the end of the hallway, her
hand over her mouth, terrified.

John reaches her.

She stares into the library.

                    JOHN
           What is it?

John turns and looks through the door.
His expression goes rigid.

                                        CUT TO:

INT. LIBRARY. NIGHT.

John and Charlotte move into the room.

The library and its contents have been completely
ransacked, destroyed. Books have been thrown off
the shelves, the table turned over, chairs piled
on top of each other.

John stops in the center of the room.

Charlotte stands behind him.

Charlotte clutches her hands together. She steps slowly through the wreckage.

> CHARLOTTE
> (quietly)
> Sarah, honey are you here?

John picks through the mess.

> JOHN
> I don't think Sarah would do something like this.

Charlotte continues to speak like a prayer.

> CHARLOTTE
> Do you want to tell us something darling? Daddy and I are here, Sarah, if you can hear me, say something.

Charlotte STOPS.

> CHARLOTTE (CONT'D)
> (shocked)
> John.

John rushes to her.

On the wall. Scrawled in a dark wet substance, is the word...

RUN

                                    CUT TO:

EXT. FRONT OF WAKEFIELD HOUSE. NEXT MORNING.

Quiet.

The Wakefield house sits in the morning light.
Charlotte emerges from the front door and moves
across the lawn.

A carriage pulls towards the house.

It stops.

The door to the carriage opens and Jennie
emerges.

Both sisters fall into each other's arms.

(Dale Dickey as Jennie Gilman)

                    CHARLOTTE
          I missed you.

Jennie smiles.

A woman, MISS CATHERINE SAYER, emerges from the
carriage with the help of the DRIVER.

                    MISS SAYER
          Thank you.

John steps out of the front door. He walks over
the porch towards the carriage.

The driver takes two bags out of the back
compartment.

John slows and tries to make out who the woman
is.

                    JENNIE
               (to Charlotte)
          This is Miss Sayer.

                    MISS SAYER
          Good morning.

                    CHARLOTTE
               (beat)
          Good morning.

                    MISS SAYER
          I have heard so much about you.

Charlotte gives a slight smile.

John reaches them.

                    JENNIE
          John. This is Miss Sayer.

                    JOHN
          Hello.

                    MISS SAYER
          So handsome. Jennie has told me so
          much about you, about both of you.

Miss Sayer smiles. She abruptly breaks away and
moves past them.

                    MISS SAYER (CONT'D)
          Well.

Miss Sayer looks at the house, then turns back to
them. Her age is indeterminable, but she is
clearly the oldest of the group.

We can barely hear what Miss Sayer says over the
wind.

                    MISS SAYER (CONT'D)
               (winks at Jennie)
          It doesn't like that we've returned.

Miss Sayer turns back to the house, lifts her
dress, and begins to walk towards it.

John and Charlotte turn back to Jennie, both
tired and sarcastically amused.

                    JOHN
               (sardonically to Jennie)
          You always have the most interesting
          friends.

                    CHARLOTTE
          Jennie, what is this?

                  JENNIE
Catherine is a woman I trust. I've
known of her since my years at school.
She studies many things. Things that
would be considered to be beyond
nature.

John turns away and shakes his head.

                  JOHN
Oh well, I suppose that explains it.

                  JENNIE
I know that she can help.

                  CHARLOTTE
Jennie. So much has happened since
you've been gone. But John and I . . .
are so much better.

                  JENNIE
Then that runs counter to how you
look. You're both pale. And thin.

                  JOHN
Oh Jennie.

                  CHARLOTTE
        (in an excited whisper)
No, the mystery of this place has only
grown.

Charlotte steps closer to Jennie.

                CHARLOTTE (CONT'D)
And it is the mystery that is
exhilarating, that has brought us
closer than we could ever have
imagined . . . John and I.

Miss Sayer has already begun moving through the front door of the house.

> JOHN
> Excuse me, but she's simply wandering into the house.

John moves off.

> CUT TO:

INT. ENTRYWAY. DAY.

Miss Sayer emerges from the dining room into the foyer. Her eyes move over the contents of the house.

> MISS SAYER
> Do you know when this house was built, Mr. Weiland?

Jennie and Charlotte stand just inside the hall.

> JOHN
> (beat)
> 1792. I think a wing was added just before the war.

> JENNIE
> But we have found papers that this same family has owned many houses all throughout Europe.

> MISS SAYER
> You don't want me here. Do you?

> JOHN
> (beat)
> No. No, it's just a bit of a surprise,

that's all.

                    MISS SAYER
          She didn't tell you I was coming?

John shakes his head.

                    MISS SAYER (CONT'D)
          Would you have let me come if she did?

He stares at her.

                    MISS SAYER (CONT'D)
          I see. Do you believe that there is a
          logical explanation, for what is
          happening in this house?

John is caught off guard.

                    JOHN
          Reasonable, if not logical.

                    MISS SAYER
          Good! That is a fair start.

                    JOHN
          I just don't understand what you think
          you can do here.

                    MISS SAYER
          Jennie believes the two of you are in
          danger.

                    JOHN
               (stepping towards her)
          Jennie (beat) exaggerates.

                    CHARLOTTE
          Miss Sayer, how would you feel about a
          nice, hot cup of tea?

                    MISS SAYER
          That would be lovely, my dear.

                    JENNIE
          And I'll take your bags upstairs to
          the extra room.

HOLD ON John, standing, silent.

                                        CUT TO:

INT. THE YELLOW WALLPAPER ROOM. DAY.

A SERIES OF SHOTS:

a.) The yellow wallpaper. Miss Sayer's hand moves
into frame, moving over the pattern.

b.) Charlotte stands close to Jennie.

c.) John watches from the doorway.

                    MISS SAYER
          There is a woman behind this wall?

                         JOHN
          A woman?

                         JENNIE
          A dead woman?

                    MISS SAYER
          No.

                    CHARLOTTE
          Perhaps you're speaking of a story
          that I have been writing. It's there
          on the desk.

Miss Sayer turns to them.

                    MISS SAYER
                (firmly)
        No. (beat) The house is full.

HOLD ON John. Fear.

Miss Sayer moves away from the wall.

                    MISS SAYER (CONT'D)
        Here. They cannot leave. They will
        not.

                    CHARLOTTE
        Sarah?

                    MISS SAYER
        And others.

                                    CUT TO:

INT. DINING ROOM. NIGHT.

Everyone sits at the dining room table. Half
empty plates sit before them. A number of candles
are lit.

Miss Sayer sips her soup.

                    JOHN
        How long have you known Jennie?

                    MISS SAYER
        My dear, let's see, oh it's been just
        'round about fifteen years now . . .

                    JENNIE
        Has it been so long? Where does it go?

                    CHARLOTTE
          Jennie has never mentioned you.

Everybody glances at Charlotte in a moment of
discomfort.

That dissolves into a soft laugh.

                    CHARLOTTE (CONT'D)
          I'm so sorry, that sounded just
          terrible.

                    MISS SAYER
          No, my dear, that is perfectly fine, I
          understood what you meant. You see,
          I'm everybody's little secret. People
          aren't so quickly inclined to mention
          the friend who prefers to spend her
          leisure time hunting about in dark old
          houses and carrying on full
          conversations with a wall.

                    JENNIE
               (smiling)
          I knew nothing of this you see, until
          much later. We first met during my
          studies. Catherine was giving a
          lecture at chapel about secular rights
          and the modern woman.

John rolls his eyes.

                    CHARLOTTE
               (to Miss Sayer)
          May I ask you a question?

                    MISS SAYER
          Of course, my dear.

                    CHARLOTTE
     Could you. . . can you. . . help
     us, to speak with Sarah?

                    JOHN
     Charlotte.

Miss Sayer takes Charlotte's hand.

                    MISS SAYER
     It would be wonderful if I could, but
     I have found that in situations such
     as this (beat), no help from the
     living can be given to speak to the
     dead...only you know how to speak to
     those you love.

                    JOHN
     Then why have you come?

                    JENNIE
     John.

                    MISS SAYER
     That's all right Jennie. I'm here
     because Jennie wanted me to come. I'm
     here because a fresh perspective can
     be as useful as anything else.

                    CHARLOTTE
                (taking Miss Sayer's hand)
     I'm quite happy that you're here.
     Anything you can tell us is. . .
     greatly appreciated.

The candles flicker.

                    MISS SAYER
     I know my dear.

Miss Sayer's smile drops into a fierce gaze as she turns to John.

He sits up.

> JOHN
> What?

Her face glazes over as if hearing something in the house.

> JENNIE
> Catherine?

> MISS SAYER
> Could you fetch me my shawl Jennie.

> JENNIE
> Yes, of course.

Miss Sayer stands up. She moves away from the table and into the

>   CUT TO:

INT. ENTRYWAY. NIGHT.

She stops.

John and Charlotte follow her.

Jennie moves into the entryway from the hallway and hands Miss Sayer her shawl.

> JENNIE
> Here it is.

> MISS SAYER
> Thank you.

Miss Sayer stands still for another moment, then moves to the door and opens it.

Then steps out onto the porch.

                                        CUT TO:

EXT. FRONT PORCH. NIGHT.

John, Charlotte, and Jennie move onto the porch. John and Jennie carry lanterns from the house.

Miss Sayer has already made her way down the porch to the stairs leading to the side of the house.

Miss Sayer lifts her dress and begins walking down the steps.

                    JOHN
          What is she doing?

                    JENNIE
          I don't know.

Charlotte moves away from them and follows Miss Sayer.

                                        CUT TO:

EXT. SIDE OF THE WAKEFIELD HOUSE. NIGHT.

Miss Sayer walks through the grass and stops at the opening to the area beneath the house.

Charlotte reaches her first, then Jennie, then John.

                    JENNIE
          What is it Catherine?

Miss Sayer turns to them.

>   MISS SAYER
>   Someone lies under there.

>   CHARLOTTE
>   Why do you say that?

>   MISS SAYER
>   Because it's calling . . . to John.

John looks at her.

The area under the house is a mass of shadows and
twisted vines.

>   MISS SAYER (CONT'D)
>   (to John)
>   You know you must go there--

>   MISS SAYER (CONT'D)
>   Alone.

John hesitates for a long moment.

>   JOHN
>   The three of you should go inside.

>   CHARLOTTE
>   We are not going inside. We are
>   waiting here.

John takes the lantern.

And disappears into the darkness.

>   CUT TO:

EXT. UNDER THE HOUSE. NIGHT.

The wind moans through the pillars beneath the house.

John is drawn to a singing sound coming from the deep hole he had discovered weeks before.

He stops at the hole.

Sets his lantern on the ground.

Crouches beside it.

Listens.

The sound hums from the black cipher.

The flickering light from the lantern barely illuminates the slippery contents. Weeds and mud.

Something moves deep in the pit.

John stares down, his eyes unwavering.

It moves again.

In a strange daze, John reaches forward and begins to slide into the hole.

The glow from the lantern dims . . .

Slowly . . .

. . . And goes out.

                                        CUT TO:

EXT. SIDE OF THE WAKEFIELD HOUSE. NIGHT.

Jennie paces, her lantern swinging in the wind.

She goes to the opening to the crawl-space.

> JENNIE
> (yells into darkness)
> John?? (beat) He's been gone too long.

> CHARLOTTE
> (to Miss Sayer)
> I don't. . . like this. Why did you
> tell him he had to go alone? You said
> you were here to help us but that
> didn't mean putting us in harm's way.

Miss Sayer stares forward.

> CHARLOTTE (CONT'D)
> Speak to me.

Charlotte grabs Miss Sayer by the arms.

> CHARLOTTE (CONT'D)
> Do you believe that this is some kind
> of a game?

> JENNIE
> (panicked whisper)
> Charlotte.

Charlotte turns.

Slowly, John emerges into the glow of Jennie's
lantern. His face and body are covered in mud.
In his arms lay the limp body of a tiny—

CHILD.

Jennie and Miss Sayer rush to John and the child.
Charlotte stands frozen.

BACK TO:

John. He walks towards Charlotte slowly, as though offering the child to her.

CLOSE UP
of Charlotte.

                                        CUT TO:

INT. THE SITTING ROOM. NIGHT.

John and Charlotte rush into the sitting room with the little girl. He sets both Charlotte and Sarah on the sofa, then yanks a linen off a side table. John covers his daughter.

Jennie and Miss Sayer enter and stop a few feet from the sofa. Their faces are transfixed in horror.

                    CHARLOTTE
          I knew it, if we stayed... I knew it
          in my heart...

John uses the blanket to wipe off the mud from the child's face.

                    JENNIE
               (muttering)
          No.

Miss Sayer grips Jennie's arm.

                    MISS SAYER
          I'll get some water and a towel.

The little girl looks up to Charlotte.

                    SARAH
          Mommy.

Charlotte cries out and buries Sarah's face in
her chest.

> CHARLOTTE
> Oh God! Thank you, thank you, thank
> you.

> JOHN
> Sweetheart?

He lifts her tiny face to him.

> JOHN (CONT'D)
> (whispers)
> Am I dreaming?

> CHARLOTTE
> Did you see us here? Have you heard us
> calling to you, my angel?

> JOHN
> How--where have you been?

Sarah's large eyes turn to her father.

> SARAH
> In the fire.

> CHARLOTTE
> No honey, no, no, not anymore.

The child looks down.

> SARAH
> Not that fire, Mommy.

John's expression darkens.

Miss Sayer has rushed back into the room with a

wet cloth.

Charlotte lifts Sarah's face again.

> CHARLOTTE
> Darling no, there was no other fire.

> SARAH
> (trembling)
> Yes there is.

> JOHN
> (quietly)
> Have you been in this house?

The child sits up.

> JOHN (CONT'D)
> (gently)
> Sarah, look at me, where have you been?

> SARAH
> (tearing up)
> In Hell.

Jennie clutches her chest.

> JENNIE
> You don't mean that.

> SARAH
> I've been burning . . .in Hell.

> MISS SAYER
> (suddenly)
> Liar.

They turn to Miss Sayer. She has a terrible,
open-eyed expression on her face.

                    MISS SAYER (CONT'D)
               (hisses)
          Liar.

They turn back to the child and -- jump!

A hunched, filthy MAN sits in the spot that Sarah
was in.

His crooked finger is pointed at Charlotte.

Everybody is in shock.

                    BURN IN HELL MAN
               (groaning)
          Hell. You both will burn in Hell for
          what you're going to do.

SUDDEN WIDE SHOT

of the room. The man is gone.

John gets up from the floor.

Charlotte begins to back up towards the wall.

                    CHARLOTTE
          No.

Jennie and John turn to her.

Miss Sayer holds her hand to her chest.

                    CHARLOTTE (CONT'D)
          No.

                    JOHN
          Charlotte. Look at me.

                         CHARLOTTE
            No. (beat) No.

John goes and grabs Charlotte. She fights him.

                         CHARLOTTE (CONT'D)
            Why?! Why are they doing this to
            us?(beat) I won't. . . NO! (to John)
            You did this. It was you. You wanted
            me that night, outside. You wanted it
            to just be us. Yes. Our filthy lust.

                         JENNIE
            Charlotte!

Miss Sayer holds Jennie back.

                         CHARLOTTE
            You don't really love me.

Charlotte has backed herself into the wall.

                         JOHN
            Stop. Stop this.

                         CHARLOTTE
            She is here! Now you have seen her.
            You've all seen her. She's with that
            man in this house. (beat) I have to
            find her. I have to go, upstairs. Yes!
            You pulled her from this house.

                         JOHN
            Charlotte!

Charlotte jumps up and rushes to the front door.
John grabs her. Charlotte struggles with him.

                                        CUT TO:

INT. ENTRYWAY. NIGHT.

                CHARLOTTE
    Let me go!

                JOHN
    Jennie, get my bag.

Jennie hesitates.

                JOHN (CONT'D)
                (yelling)
    Jennie NOW!

She rushes from the room.

                CHARLOTTE
    Let go of me!

                MISS SAYER
    Charlotte, you're all wrong about
    this.

                CHARLOTTE
    You want me to believe that. I know
    you do. That is what this is all
    about. (sobbing) You brought her out!
    We can go back and get her. She's
    here! We've seen her. Please!

Jennie rushes back into the room.

                JOHN
    No honey. No. Oh God Charlotte. It was
    not Sarah. It was a trick. They are
    tricking us. They want us to stay
    here. They want us to believe that she
    is here.

>   MISS SAYER O.C.
>   Sarah is here.

Beat.

>   MISS SAYER
>   She has been with you since the moment
>   you lost her. She's even been in this
>   house.

Charlotte starts to shake violently.

>   JOHN
>   (to Miss Sayer)
>   Quiet!

Miss Sayer step closer to them.

>   MISS SAYER
>   But John is correct. That was not your
>   daughter.

Charlotte begins to lose balance, melting into
John.

>   CHARLOTTE
>   (to John)
>   I can feel her. She's so close
>   John, (beat) John.

Jennie re-enters the room with John's doctor's
bag.

EXTREME CLOSE OF CHARLOTTE AND JOHN

Charlotte whispers to him.

>   CHARLOTTE (CONT'D)
>   I can't take anymore. Not right now.
>   Not like this.

                         JOHN
            I know.

John and Jennie exchange a look.

CLOSE UP of fluid going into a syringe.

Jennie goes to John and Charlotte. She hands John
the syringe.

John injects the needle into Charlotte's arm.
Charlotte's eyes begin to close.

                    JOHN (CONT'D)
                  (to Charlotte)
            It's done now; it's done.

                    CHARLOTTE
                  (with her last strength)
            Would that I could sleep my life
            away...

                                        CUT TO:

INT. SITTING ROOM. NIGHT.

Covered by a blanket, Charlotte is unconscious on
the settee.

Both women are squeezed together on the sitting
room sofa and John sits across from them in a
chair.

The three of them struggle to stay awake. Miss
Sayer reads a book.

Gathered lanterns are set upon a little table at
the center of the room.

> JENNIE
> (to Miss Sayer)
> How did you know?

She looks up at Jennie.

> JENNIE (CONT'D)
> To go under the house.

Miss Sayer gently lays her book in her lap.

> MISS SAYER
> It sounds like singing. When I hear
> it, I follow, but I never know what
> I'll find. The rest, I rely on
> instinct.

There is a long silence in the room.

> JENNIE
> (quietly, to anyone)
> Are we safe in here?

> MISS SAYER
> Yes, we are safe.

John stares at the lantern flame and tries to
keep his eyes open.

> JOHN
> (mutters)
> We leave in the morning.

                                        CUT TO:

INT. SITTING ROOM. DAY.

HARSH sunlight fills the room.

John awakes. He is pale, groggy and can barely

move. He stands, and moves beside Charlotte on the sofa. Gently, John moves the hair off of her forehead and lifts her hand to take her pulse. He leans into her.

                    JOHN
          Charlotte? Can you hear me?

                  CHARLOTTE
            (her eyes still closed)
          Yes I can hear you, John.

Jennie jerks awake.

                    JENNIE
          What's happening? Is she all right?
          What time is it?

                    JOHN
          She's fine.

John turns over his shoulder to Jennie.

                    JOHN (CONT'D)
                  (to Jennie)
          Are you all right?

                    JENNIE
          Fine, yes, I just couldn't stop
          sleeping. Where is Catherine?

John looks to the sofa. Miss Sayer's shawl lays
over the arm. Miss Sayer is gone.

Jennie gets up and goes to Charlotte.

                    JENNIE (CONT'D)
          Charlotte, honey, is there anything I
          can get for you?

                    CHARLOTTE
                  (eyes closed)
          No, thank you.

Jennie turns and steps out of the room.

Charlotte opens her eyes and looks at John.

                    CHARLOTTE (CONT'D)
          I had the most terrible dreams. You
          were...old and looked so very, very
          sad.

Jennie walks back into the room.

                    JENNIE
          It's one thirty in the afternoon. And
          I cannot seem to find Catherine.

                                        CUT TO:

INT. SEWING ROOM. DAY.

Charlotte and Jennie pack a bag at the table.
Charlotte is weak and sits down. Jennie reaches
for her with a look of concern. Charlotte waves
at her with an "I'm fine" gesture.

John enters.

> JOHN
> I've looked everywhere. If she's here,
> then I can't find her. Is it possible
> that she would have already left?

> JENNIE
> No, she wouldn't just leave. Not
> without telling us, leaving some kind
> of a note.

> CHARLOTTE
> Perhaps she's already gone into town,
> to secure us a carriage.

> JOHN
> Well we're not going to wait around to
> found out. If she has gone to town
> then I'm bound to run into her. Are
> the both of you ready?

Jennie takes the bag from the table.

Charlotte stands.

> JENNIE
> We're ready.

> CUT TO:

EXT. FRONT PORCH. DAY.

John, Charlotte, and Jennie emerge from the house.

John shuts the door behind them.

> CHARLOTTE
> (weakly)
> John.

She begins to collapse. John catches her.

> JOHN
> All right. Come on.

John, carrying the bag, leads his wife, with Jennie's help, away from the house, and down the steps.

> CUT TO:

EXT. FRONT OF WAKEFIELD HOUSE. DAY.

They walk to a small stone seat at the end of the walkway.

> JENNIE
> John, I'm worried that something has happened to Catherine, this is not like her.

John helps Charlotte to sit on the bench.

> JOHN
> (to Jennie)
> Listen, some terrible things have happened since we've been here, but so far, I know nobody has been truly hurt. I feel sure that she is just

fine.

Jennie opens a parasol to protect them from the late day sun.

>   JOHN (CONT'D)
>   (to both women)
>   It should take me three quarters of an
>   hour to get to town, hopefully less
>   back, depending on if I can find a
>   carriage. But under no circumstances
>   do I want you or Charlotte to go into
>   the house.

>   JENNIE
>   Finally, we're in agreement on
>   something.

They exchange a look.

>   JENNIE (CONT'D)
>   She'll be fine with me.

>   JOHN
>   (tender smile)
>   I know. She always was.

John leans down to Charlotte and whispers to her.

>   JOHN (CONT'D)
>   Try to rest.

John starts walking off. He turns back while walking.

>   JOHN (CONT'D)
>   Stay close together, and away from
>   that house. I'll be back soon.

Charlotte jumps up.

                    CHARLOTTE
          John!

She walks quickly to him.

                    CHARLOTTE (CONT'D)
          I just want to tell you, I wanted to
          say. That I've been so foolish. And
          selfish for so long.

John starts to shake his head "No".

                    CHARLOTTE (CONT'D)
              (motioning him to wait)
          Please . . .I haven't been seeing
          anything clearly, even, before. I
          hadn't been seeing . . .you. (looking
          down) why have you stayed with me?

He touches her chin, she looks up at him.

                    JOHN
          Because I love you.

Her eyes grow wide. A strange reserve passes over
them. John gives a sad smile and turns away.

Charlotte slowly makes her way back to the bench.
She is just a few paces from Jennie when she
turns.

Running to John.

                    CHARLOTTE
          John!

He spins in her direction and catches her in his

arms.

They embrace in a kiss, that could set the world
on fire.

John holds her face, covering one another in a
flurry of pecks and hugs.

> JOHN
> God, I love. I love you, I love you.

John kisses her. Charlotte's face is turned up to
God as if a terrible weight had been lifted from
her. They pull away from each other slowly.

He looks down to her. The tiniest hint of smile
touches the corner of his mouth.

They part, holding each other's hands until the
last possible moment.

FADE OUT:

EXT. DRY LAKE BED. DAY.

John's tiny figure walks across the barren land.

CUT TO:

EXT. FRONT OF WAKEFIELD HOUSE. DAY.

The wind blows through the grass in the front
yard.

Charlotte and Jennie sit on the stone seat and
wait for John.

CUT TO:

EXT. FRONT OF WAKEFIELD HOUSE. DAY. LATER

Charlotte and Jennie sit at the stone seat beyond
the house. Sweat beads over their brows under the
hypnotic sun.

Jennie offers the black lace parasol to
Charlotte. Charlotte takes it. She sits down next
to her sister. She holds the parasol over both of
them.

                                        CUT TO:

The trees. Rustling, and shifting.

                                        CUT TO:

EXT. SIDE OF THE HOUSE. DAY.

Charlotte moves the parasol away from her face.
She stands at the base of the house. Her
perspective is on the window to the yellow
wallpaper room.

Jennie, still sitting, pulls a book from the bag
while watching her sister.

Charlotte turns away from the house and walks
back towards Jennie.

                                        CUT TO:

EXT. FOREST GROVE. DAY.

John walks along the path towards town.

                                        CUT TO:

EXT. FRONT OF WAKEFIELD HOUSE. DAY.

Charlotte's feet crunch over the dry grass.

She stops.

And looks down into the dirt.

A shoe lies in the weeds.

The wind kicks up and begins to moan.

Cautiously, Charlotte picks up the shoe.

She quickly recognizes it as Miss Sayer's shoe.

Charlotte looks up in the direction of the two
mysterious graves in the tall grass beyond the
front walkway.

She moves towards them.

Jennie stands up in the distance. She sets down
her book and heads towards Charlotte.

As Charlotte nears the graves, she can just
barely see the disturbed earth through the tall
grass.

She stops.

Jennie runs up alongside her, then turns her face
away in terror.

Miss Sayer lies in the opened coffin. Her body
has been half covered in dirt and her hands are
clenched like gnarled claws. Her hat covers her
face, but one can just see the outline of her

profile.

WIDE SHOT

of Jennie and Charlotte and the Wakefield house.
Charlotte holds Jennie's hand, but can't take her
eyes away.

Then, over the wind--

a wild dog howls.

CUT TO:

EXT. TOWN. DAY.

WIDE SHOT

of John walking across the center of town. The
streets are completely empty.

Dust kicks up in the late day sun.

Curious figures seem to adorn each door.

Wooden crosses.

John squints to see them.

He wanders, confused.

In the distance, movement.

A young girl rushes between two wooden buildings.
She carries a brown bag.

John tries to get a vantage point at which to see
her.

She vanishes.

John scurries through alleyways.

The girl appears again, walking fast.

She disappears down an alley.

John follows.

The girl approaches a door.

John watches her, then walks up to her fast.

                    JOHN
          Excuse me!

The girl swings around, screams.

The bag falls to the ground, the groceries
spilling out.

She presses herself against the door.

It is Mrs. Tremayne from the tea party.

                    JOHN (CONT'D)
          You were at our house.

She says nothing.

                    MRS. TREMAYNE
               (eyes glazed in terror)
          What are you doing here?

                    JOHN
          What?

                    MRS. TREMAYNE
          I can't speak with you.

                    JOHN
        Why? Why can't you speak with me?

                    MRS. TREMAYNE
        You have to leave here!

                    JOHN
        Why?

                    MRS. TREMAYNE
        I can't. (beat) We need you there,
        please.

                    JOHN
        Who does? Where is everyone?

                    MRS. TREMAYNE
        We can't let it come to town.

                    JOHN
        Let what come to town?

                    MRS. TREMAYNE
                (whimpering)
        We can't let it come into town! If not
                    MRS. TREMAYNE (CONT'D)
        --you, then us.

John lets go of the girl and backs up.

She stares back at him.

John turns and runs.

                                    CUT TO:

EXT. PORCH. DAY.

Jennie and Charlotte back onto the porch. They stare forward, terrified.

A wild dog stands just beyond the front gate. It is matted with blood and dirt.

Another wild dog emerges from the bushes. It moves towards them from the opposite direction.

Jennie and Charlotte back into the front door of the Wakefield house.

The animals move forward.

Jennie reaches behind her and opens the door. They both rush inside and shut the door.

                              CUT TO:

EXT. FOREST GROVE. DAY.

John runs over the dirt road. The setting sun is flaring down to a burnt orange.

                              CUT TO:

INT. ENTRYWAY. DAY.

Charlotte and Jennie stand in the entryway. Jennie glances out the side window.

                    CHARLOTTE
              They're still there.

A ghostly laugh.

The women turn.

A terrible creaking sound from the left side of

the house.

Further off, some glass breaks.

Jennie takes Charlotte by the arm.

> JENNIE
> I think we can get out the back.

>> CUT TO:

EXT. ROAD. DAY.

The sun hangs low on the horizon and the strange glow reflects off the nearby mountains.

The long road to the house is empty.

John slows down, panting, and stops.

Takes in a breath.

Looks back to the sun.

Then to the road ahead.

A man! -- standing before him.

John jumps. He immediately recognizes him as the man shoveling rats in the road when they first arrived.

> RAT MAN
> You can't go back now. It's too late.

John moves around the man, horrified. He glances over the field towards the house.

> RAT MAN O.C.
> Spare yourself.

John shakes his head, then turns and stumbles
into the field.

                    RAT MAN
                  (hollering)
              You're too late!

John turns back.

The road is empty.

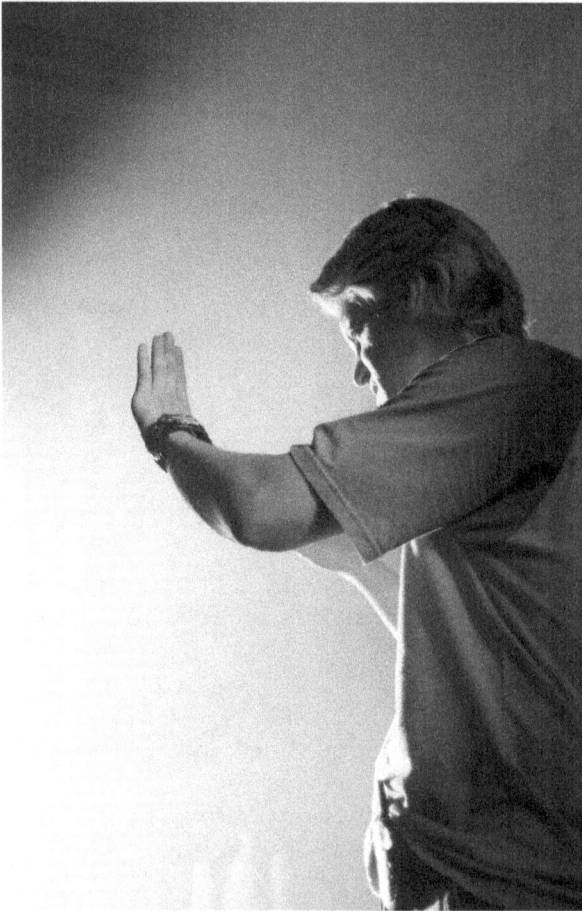

(Logan composes a shot.)

CUT TO:

INT. FIRST HALLWAY. TWILIGHT.

Jennie and Charlotte rush into the hallway.

Step by step.

Sounds.

Everywhere.

Moving chairs.

Doors.

Both women stop.

The hall stretches out before them.

CUT TO:

EXT. FIELD. TWILIGHT.

EXTREME CLOSE UP

John just reaches the large field where the Wakefield house looms.

He is drenched in sweat.

CUT TO:

INT. SECOND HALLWAY. TWILIGHT.

Jennie reaches the entrance to the second hallway. Charlotte is right behind her.

Jennie peaks into the second hallway.

Empty.

She moves into it.

And turns back to Charlotte.

But Charlotte is gone.

Panicked, Jennie retraces her steps.

                    JENNIE
          Charlotte?

The first hallway is empty.

                    JENNIE (CONT'D)
          Charlotte?!

Jennie looks this way and that!

                                        CUT TO:

INT. THE YELLOW WALLPAPER ROOM. TWILIGHT.

We slowly move over the wooden planked floor
towards the rusted metal bed at the end of the
room. Dappled golden light flickers through the
window over the dull yellow paper.

With the sound of a CRACK, a small door tears
open in the wall.

On the other side.

Blackness.

                                        CUT TO:

INT. JENNIE'S ROOM. TWILIGHT.

Jennie throws open the door.

> JENNIE
> Charlotte!

CUT TO:

INT. SECOND HALLWAY. TWILIGHT.

Jennie reaches the door to the library.

She slowly pushes it open.

The room is partially revealed.

Long shadows shroud the library.

Jennie enters.

> JENNIE
> (whispers)
> Charlotte?

CUT TO:

INT. LIBRARY. TWILIGHT.

Jennie moves to the center of the room. She is dwarfed by the Wakefield portrait above her. Something moves in the corner.

Jennie puts her hand on a small table to steady herself.

A lantern falls.

Shatters!

She jumps.

Then presses her hand to her chest.

Jennie moves to the large desk.

Something crouches in the corner.

                    JENNIE
          Charlotte?

A dark mass.

It twists towards her like an animal.

Then rises.

To full height.

Jennie's expression changes.

To terror.

                                        CUT TO:

EXT. FRONT OF WAKEFIELD HOUSE. TWILIGHT.

John reaches the stone seat. He bends over,
clutching his side, and panting.

The bag and parasol are abandoned.

John looks up to the house.

                                        CUT TO:

EXT. THE WAKEFIELD HOUSE. TWILIGHT.

The house stands against the sky.

A piercing SCREAM!

WE PULL IN FAST

to John as he looks up to the house.

                                        CUT TO:

INT. ENTRYWAY. NIGHT

The front door is thrown open.

John runs in--

Stops.

                    JOHN
          Charlotte?

Nothing.

                    JOHN (CONT'D)
          Jennie?

The house is NOW completely silent.

John moves into the sitting room.

Empty.

                                        CUT TO:

INT. JOHN AND CHARLOTTE'S ROOM. TWILIGHT.

He opens the door.

No one.

                                        CUT TO:

INT. SECOND HALLWAY. TWILIGHT.

John moves into the second hallway.

The library door opens.

Just sees it.

He quickly moves over the floor and to the door.

                    JOHN
              Charlotte?

John pushes open the door and enters.

                              CUT TO:

INT. LIBRARY. TWILIGHT.

Flies buzz over the desk.

Dark blood is spattered across the wall. Bits of
lace and Jennie's dress are pressed into the
bloodied floor.

John stares down at the remains.

He steps back.

                    JOHN
                (under his breath)
              Jennie.

His eyes widen.

He turns.

Runs.

Out into the hall.

                                        CUT TO:

INT. JENNIE'S ROOM. TWILIGHT.

John throws open the door.

Frantic!

                    JOHN
              Charlotte!?

Runs back out into the hall.

An Eighteenth Century Woman stands in the hall.
Her dress is faded, her face deathly.

                    EIGHTEENTH CENTURY WOMAN
              We told you to leave.

                                   CUT BACK TO:

John. Stunned.

Blinks.

The woman is gone.

John stands for another moment, then RUNS into .
. .

                                        CUT TO:

INT. SITTING ROOM. TWILIGHT.

Wind billows the curtains away from the window.
John dashes into the room and STOPS!

Sarah, sits on the settee. Her little feet dangle

above the floor.

> SARAH
> I'm sorry, Papa.

John is shaking with emotion.

> JOHN
> Honey. Where's. . . where's your
> mommy?

Sarah's eyes move across the sitting room. Her gaze fixes on the closed, wooden doors that lead to the dining room.

John follows her eyes.

He looks back to her.

Gone.

Curtains blow over the empty sofa.

John walks through the room and into the...

> CUT TO:

INT. ENTRYWAY. TWILIGHT.

As John approaches the door he can hear a heavy chair move, on the other side.

John listens.

He stops at the point where the doors meet.

A sliver of red sunlight peers through, onto his face.

He carefully opens the doors.

The dining room is ablaze with the dying colors of dusk.

John stands.

JOHN POV
of the table. The large glass centerpiece vase sits in the middle of the table, obscuring the man sitting just behind.

Gnarled, soiled hands rest calmly on the surface.

CUT TO:

INT. DINING ROOM. TWILIGHT.

John slowly steps to the side . . .

To see the man.

Wakefield is revealed.

He sits in the chair at the table.

His head is covered with thin, gray hair. His skin has a sickly yellow tint. His lips are drawn back from a mouth filled with rotting teeth, and his eyes, are burnt yellow orbs that reek of disease.

Wakefield moves one long, thin hand gently over the table.

                    JOHN
          You are not a phantom.

                    WAKEFIELD
                 (old Dutch)
          I am a man. But poisoned.

```
                    JOHN
          What?

                    JOHN (CONT'D)
          Wakefield.

                    WAKEFIELD
                    (English)
          How strong is your love, Dr. Weiland?

                    JOHN
          Where is my wife?
```

(Aric confronts Wakefield)

```
                    WAKEFIELD
          How strong is your love Dr. Weiland?
```

John looks at Wakefield closer. Two small canine
teeth touch the edges of Wakefield's lips.

                         JOHN
          What are you? (beat) Why are you in
          this house? What could you possibly
          want from--

BOOM!

Wakefield explodes out from behind the table. His
attack on John is so sudden, everything goes to
black.

                                        CUT TO:

Darkness. The deep sound of the ocean, churning.
Far in the distance is the echo of a harpsichord.

                                        CUT TO:

WAKEFIELD POV

of a dirty knight in banged up armor. He sits
before a tiny fire.

The knight turns to camera as he hears something
coming from out of the trees.

He stands as our POV moves towards him, an
expression of bewilderment covering his face.

                                        CUT TO:

INT. EIGHTEENTH CENTURY PARLOR. NIGHT.

Lit by a hundred burning candles.

In a large, gold brocade chair, sits a VENETIAN
WOMAN. Her face is painted white and a tall
powdered wig adorns her head. The rest of her
body is limp and nude.

She stares unflinchingly at us.

At her feet lay a nude, EFFETE YOUNG MAN.

He also turns his gaze to us.

                                        CUT TO:

INT. THE YELLOW WALLPAPER ROOM. DAY. FLASHBACK.
Wakefield is bent over Charlotte. His mouth is
locked onto her arm. He drinks her blood as he
gently moves his hands over her body, the nails
barely grazing the skin.

                                   DISSOLVE TO:

INT. JOHN AND CHARLOTTE'S ROOM. NIGHT.

John wakes up to see Wakefield feeding on his
leg. He then slips back into unconsciousness.

                                        CUT TO:

INT. SITTING ROOM. DAY. FLASHBACK.

SHAKY POV

of John's hand pulling soil out of the crate from
the sitting room.

                    JENNIE O.C.
              . . . found it this morning. What
              would they use it for?

                                        CUT TO:

EXT. DIRT ROAD. DAY. FLASHBACK.

CLOSE on pile of rotting rats. A billow of smoke

curls up from the pit beside them.

                                        CUT TO:

EXT. TOWN. DAY. FLASHBACK.

ANGLE ON deserted town.

Doors adorned with crosses.

                                        CUT TO:

EXT. WAKEFIELD HOUSE. NIGHT.

Fog envelopes the Wakefield house.

                                        CUT TO:

EXT. SUN. DAY.

The giant, fiery sun burns out into darkness.

                                        CUT TO:

INT. DINING ROOM. NEXT MORNING.

John awakes. Disoriented.

Blue morning light fills the house.

He leans up.

Charlotte lay on the floor, a few feet from him.
He crawls to her. He checks for her breath.

Nothing. John moves his head to her chest and
listens.

No heartbeat.

John pulls away. His face collapses.

                                              CLOSE ON
Charlotte.

Her eyes open.

John's expression widens in shock.

                        CHARLOTTE
            John.

                        JOHN
            My love?

                        CHARLOTTE
            John. I'm so sorry.

He is confused.

Suddenly, the sound of the front door . . .

Opening.

John turns.

From around the corner, Mr. Hendricks emerges
from the entryway.

He walks slowly and deliberately, past John.
Then stops.

He looks down to the disintegrated mass of ash
and muddy robes that was once Wakefield.

Mr. Hendricks stands over the remains for a long
time before he speaks.

> MR. HENDRICKS
> She's dead. Her heart will never beat
> again. But... the disease... will keep
> her body animate. (beat) I do not know
> why, and as so far as I am aware, no
> one has ever known.

He turns back to the remains of Wakefield.

> MR. HENDRICKS (CONT'D)
> We have carried this thing for just
> short of three centuries.

Mr. Hendricks shifts his eyes to meet John's.
John's stare shifts to Wakefield, then down to
Charlotte.

Mr. Hendricks' cane raps a terrible BANG on the
wood floor.

John jerks up to see Mr. Hendricks approaching
him.

> MR. HENDRICKS (CONT'D)
> You are going to have to make a choice
> now, John. You can leave her here,
> abandoned, without aid, and she will
> be trapped inside that flesh
> indefinitely... able to think, to
> dream, to hear... but helpless. And
> you very soon will die.

Mr. Hendricks' face warms over.

> MR. HENDRICKS (CONT'D)
> Or, you can bring to this house, those
> from whom she can feed, and in turn
> she can feed you. (beat) You will be
> bound together in this cycle until she
> gives it to another. I tell you these

things because I made a promise to do
so...if it came to that.

He begins to cross the dining room towards the
front door.

> MR. HENDRICKS (CONT'D)
> Time is short now, so listen to me
> closely.

Mr. Hendricks stops short of the large, open
door.

> MR. HENDRICKS (CONT'D)
> She will be useless during the day.
> You will not. But she'll be able to do
> miraculous things during the night,
> and you will not.

He waves his hand in a odd gesture.

> MR. HENDRICKS (CONT'D)
> The rest, you will come to know.

Mr. Hendricks begins to exit, then stops.

> MR. HENDRICKS (CONT'D)
> Oh, one other thing, for reasons I do
> not understand, she will be able to
> effect and manipulate the wills of
> some animals. Rodents and wolves,
> appear to be the most susceptible.

John watches him, stunned.

Mr. Hendricks points his cane out the door.

> MR. HENDRICKS (CONT'D)
> You may use that second grave
> now,(beat) for the sister.

Mr. Hendricks takes a long beat as he looks down
to John.

> MR. HENDRICKS (CONT'D)
> In homes we were all born. In homes we
> all die, or hope to die.

He exits.

Silence.

Dizzy and broken, John sits with Charlotte in his
arms.

> CUT TO:

INT. SECOND HALLWAY. DAY.

Silhouetted, John carries Charlotte's limp body
through the hallway.

> CUT TO:

INT. THE YELLOW WALLPAPER ROOM. DAY.

John holds Charlotte in his arms.

The door in the wall is open.

He stares at it.

Then down to Charlotte.

Charlotte looks up to him. Her eyes, pulled back
into dark holes, her skin stretched over her
narrow face. It is not his Charlotte, but
Wakefield's Charlotte. Her countenance has
changed and has taken on similar features to that
of Wakefield's. The hands, the nails, the drawn
back eyes.

                    JOHN
          Darling?

Charlotte looks too weak to say anything. Tears
move down her face.

                  CHARLOTTE
          We don't ever have to leave her now.

Charlotte's feet dangle. Her body is almost
completely exsanguinated. Her bloodied dress
shifts slightly in the breeze.

Tears move down his face in the shifting light as
he carries her to the attic tomb.

John kneels.

He gently places her frail body on a bed of rich
soil, in the darkness, behind the yellow

wallpaper.

John looks at her.

The lantern illuminates her sunken eyes.

CLOSE UP
of John.

>   JOHN
>   (whispers)
>   Rest. Until nightfall.

Charlotte looks at him and nods.

She tries to speak.

John leans in to listen to her. She whispers to
him.

He nods.

John backs away from the door. He takes a long
last look.

ANGLE ON

Charlotte in the darkened crawl space. She looks
back at him, resolved. Her eyes open, John closes
the door on her.

As the door closes, and the light diminishes, we
see Charlotte's eyes in the darkness. Glimmering
slightly. Knowing. . . what she has become,
what she is.

>   CUT TO:

INT. LIBRARY. DAY.

John walks into the destroyed library. His face
is weighed down, and his clothes are still matted
and crumpled.

He goes to a large chair and sits beneath the
Wakefield portrait.

He stares forward for a long time, then slowly
draws a book from the chair beside him.

He opens the book on his lap.

And begins to read.

An echo.

Far off in the house.

John looks up in the direction of the sound.
He moves methodically across the room and to the
door.

He steps into the hallway.

And stops.

Footsteps approach.

HOLD on John.

At the far end of the hall, a figure rounds the
corner.

It is--

JOHN WEILAND. His clothes are noticeably modern.
His face and hair have not changed. His gait is
confident and quiet as he passes the spot he

stood . . .

100 years before.

John stops.

Hovers for a moment.

He looks down to the second hallway.

A young man stands there.

It is TRAVIS PRESTON, 30.

> TRAVIS
> It looks great. Have you showed it to
> anyone else?

> JOHN
> Not yet.

COLLEEN PRESTON, 35, moves into the hallway to
her husband.

> TRAVIS
> All right? What's the deal? How can
> you afford to rent it so cheap?

> JOHN
> Well, the owners paid for the house
> long ago.

> COLLEEN
> So we benefit! (beat) We have our own
> furniture. Do you think the owners
> would put this stuff in storage?

> JOHN
> I'm afraid not. You can add, but you

can't take away. (to Travis) What do
                JOHN (CONT'D)
you do for work?

                    TRAVIS
          She's the one with the exciting
          occupation.

                    COLLEEN
          No. I'm a writer. Social commentary--
          it's nothing.

                    JOHN
          My wife is a writer.

                    COLLEEN
          Really? What's her name?

                    JOHN
          You wouldn't know her. She uses many--
          pen names. Her sister had a lot to do
          with her work after she died.

                                    CUT TO:

INT. THE YELLOW WALLPAPER ROOM. DAY.

                    TRAVIS
          I suppose we couldn't take down the
          wallpaper.

Colleen stands by the small windows. The room is
barren.

John looks at him with a smile saying 'of course
not'.

Travis stands near the stairs.

John leans against the wall (where Charlotte lays

behind). He looks at them, but says nothing.
There is a tinge of a smile on the corner of his
lips.

> COLLEEN
> No, no. Travis, this can be the
> nursery. It's perfect.

> TRAVIS
> Oh Colleen. It's a little out of the
> way, don't you think?

> COLLEEN
> Oh, it will be lovely.

Travis turns to John.

> TRAVIS
> We're expecting. . .a daughter.

> JOHN
> (beat)
> Congratulations.

WE HOLD ON JOHN as the camera moves in to him. He
stands against the wall as we slowly FADE DOWN
on John's face

and the yellow wallpaper.

THE END.

Special Thanks to Mary, the Grip.

www.ingramcontent.com/pod-product-compliance
Lightning Source LLC
LaVergne TN
LVHW051238080426
835513LV00016B/1655